PENGUIN BOOKS

THE CUSTOM OF THE COU

John McRae is Special Professor of Language in Literature Study at the University of Nottingham, and Professeur Invité at the Université d'Avignon et des Pays de Vaucluse. He is joint series editor with Professor Ronald Carter of Penguin Student Editions, for which he has edited *Jane Eyre*, *A Christmas Carol*, *A Passage to India*, *The Garden Party and Other Stories*, *The Strange Case of Doctor Jekyll and Mr Hyde* and *The Hound of the Baskervilles*. His other publications include *Literature with a small 'l'*, *The Language of Poetry* and *The Routledge History of Literature in English*, the last with Ronald Carter.

The author wants to thank the following for help and support in the writing of these Notes:

Helen Woodeson at Penguin France;

Kathy John, Laura Barber and Andrea Rayner at Penguin UK;

Valerie Durow at the School of English Studies, Nottingham University;

Jeremy Hunter at La Cabanié;

Rajen Ramiah at Villa Puteri, Kuala Lumpur.

Penguin Study Notes

EDITH WHARTON

The Custom of the Country

JOHN McRAE

PENGUIN BOOKS

PENGUIN BOOKS

Published by the Penguin Group
Penguin Books Ltd, 27 Wrights Lane, London W8 5TZ, England
Penguin Putnam Inc., 375 Hudson Street, New York, New York 10014, USA
Penguin Books Australia Ltd, Ringwood, Victoria, Australia
Penguin Books Canada Ltd, 10 Alcorn Avenue, Toronto, Ontario, Canada M4V 3B2
Penguin Books (NZ) Ltd, Private Bag 102902, NSMC, Auckland, New Zealand

Penguin Books Ltd, Registered Offices: Harmondsworth, Middlesex, England

First published 2000
10 9 8 7 6 5 4 3 2 1

Set in 10/12.5 pt PostScript Monotype Ehrhardt
Typeset by Rowland Phototypesetting Ltd, Bury St Edmunds, Suffolk
Printed in England by Clays Ltd, St Ives plc

Contents

To the Student

This study guide aims to offer the reader a chapter-by-chapter guide through the novel, picking up and elaborating many of the points raised in the Introduction, and again in Critical Viewpoints. Readers are strongly recommended to read the novel for themselves first, without making reference to the Notes, in order to enjoy the plot and its surprises, its inevitability and its irony, without interference. Second and further readings will be enriched with the accompaniment of the Commentary and Notes, although it is up to the individual reader to decide on particular emphases and interpretations, and to pick out his or her own favourite 'useful quotations'. The novel is full of quotable lines, and the commentary only selects one or two for each chapter.

Of course the Notes cannot pick up every point worth noting and analysing – it is hoped the reader will find many other points of interest, quotations to savour, and interpretations to debate. It is not necessary to agree with the Notes – they are never the final word!

The Notes later offer points for discussion and analysis in order to help readers develop their ideas on the issues the novel raises and the ways in which the contrasts, for example, between American and French society are brought out.

Historical background and some biographical detail are also given, together with suggestions for Further Reading which go beyond what can be done in a brief study guide.

All page references are to the Penguin Twentieth-Century Classics edition of *The Custom of the Country*, with an Introduction by the novelist Anita Brookner.

Introduction

Edith Wharton was fifty when she wrote *The Custom of the Country* and was to be divorced from her husband, Edward Robbins Wharton, in the same year as the novel was published, 1913. They had been married some twenty-eight years earlier, in 1885, when she was twenty-three. Her husband was twelve years her senior. According to Louis Auchincloss, 'she had always scribbled, but then, perhaps to relieve the tensions of an unhappy marriage, she began to write'.

Although it is usually dangerous to assume close biographical links between an author and the circumstances of her life, it is no accident that one of the main themes of *The Custom of the Country* is divorce. The critic, Malcolm Bradbury, goes so far as to say that the 'custom' itself refers to 'regular divorce', although that is rather limiting. The novel has a wide range of themes and concerns, of which divorce is one, albeit a very major one.

It is Edith Wharton's most brilliantly ironic novel, with a complex plot, full of twists and surprises, moving back and forward in time, and with a wide range of characters, bringing together the two societies she herself knew best – the high society of America, and New York in particular, and the society of France, where she made her home from 1910. Auchincloss states that 'she wanted a society that was disciplined as well as charming, intellectual as well as lively. For her it could be found only in France.'

The Custom of the Country is the central novel of what critics like to call Wharton's 'major period', which begins in 1905 with *The House of Mirth*. That novel is in many ways a tragic counterpart to *The Custom of the Country*, with many shared themes, such as the 'Invaders' who come from the hinterland of America to intrude upon the settled society of Washington Square and Fifth Avenue in New York. The theme of beauty and the closely related concern with money and debt are common to the two novels. And the heroines, Lily Bart and Undine Spragg are in many ways sisters. Undine, however, is not New York born, and that is in every way her problem. It may also, by the end of the novel, be her salvation. For Lily is a tragic heroine – she is literally torn to pieces by the conflict within New York society between everything it would like to be and everything it is not. Society has to destroy her.

Undine Spragg is perhaps more naïve, but infinitely more of a survivor. She is associated with frontier territory and new boundaries, often undefined. She comes to New York from Apex, the uncharted new and growing city somewhere in the mid-West which comes to represent all that is corrupt about business and all that is naïve in society. New York is alien territory, but she is determined to make her mark in that society. Her career, through marriage and sheer ruthless selfishness, takes her to the heights of Parisian society too, and she survives and prospers, never seeing the savage irony of her success and never escaping the shadow of the ever-present Apex, the past from which her present derives. At the end of the book, as she prepares to welcome her glittering guests, there is one new 'tiny black cloud' on the horizon. Undine will never be wholly satisfied, and her story looks towards a future in which her son, Paul Marvell, will be 'the richest boy in America . . .' That prospect must strike every reader as a desolate and worrying one for Paul, a poor little rich kid long before that kind of character became a stereotype of the twentieth century.

Edith Wharton is a modernist in her concept of society, of power relationships, of the roles of women, and in her perceptions of humanity and its emptiness, its 'heart of darkness', to use Joseph Conrad's title. But she is a traditionalist too. *The Custom of the Country*, despite the modernity of its themes and its topical references to telephones and automobiles, also harks back to the previous century's literature in some significant ways: it has a taste of Dickens in some of the characters, such as the eternal gossip Mrs Heeny, with her bag full of newspaper clippings; it also echoes *Bleak House* and the emptiness of Lady Dedlock's life in the St Désert scenes; and it encompasses the

Henry James of *Washington Square*, but goes far beyond James in its perceptions of the seamier sides of life.

Edith Wharton has often been rather misleadingly associated with James, and her reputation has been too closely allied with his. She is quite a different kind of writer, much more concerned with the machinations of society, with what might be described as 'real' life. *The Custom of the Country* indeed frequently echoes Balzac with his concept of 'the human comedy' and his concentration on the more negative aspects of human motivation. Irony and the clever variation of narratorial perspective is Wharton's mode. She is unafraid to experiment with modern narrative techniques in order to get inside the thoughts of her characters, and she does so with conviction and ease. She never writes a sentence that is longer than it needs to be, she never stretches a paragraph, as Henry James certainly does (and Edith Wharton criticized his later novels for this 'over-wordiness' of style). Her writing flows, for the reader, with an ease and rapidity that give her novels a marvellous fluency, a raciness almost. The only slowing down is in the desolation of the St Désert scenes, the veritable calm before the storm, the darkest hour before Undine's new dawn.

There is a sense in which the America of this novel is unfinished: the new places and states like South Dakota and the wonderfully named Opake, Nebraska, are beyond the pale. There are even states that 'don't have a name yet'. This is a society still in a condition bordering on an 'age of innocence' – which was to be the title of Wharton's 1920 masterpiece, looking back on a lost world before the cataclysm. If American society is unfinished, French society is stultifying in its ancient modes and traditions. Each society falsifies the other and has a mistaken idea of the other. The judgements are themselves an indication of the distance between America and France, in terms of time and of space. It is a comedy of mismatching, far removed from Henry James's aesthetic appreciation of European values and ways. The customs of the country are different, and, in many ways, to echo Kipling, 'ne'er the twain shall meet', although of course they do, with varying degrees of success, acceptance, failure and disappointment.

The common currency is, of course, money. Money is at the root of absolutely everything in this novel. But it is new money that wins: the society of entrepreneurs and risk-takers, the whiz-kids of Wall Street and the new industrial barons. Old money loses out, and old standards suffer in consequence. Hard work and a good degree of chance are what lead to riches. Nobody even thinks of money buying happiness. And love is hardly mentioned. Values fall somewhere by the wayside, and have to be picked up and re-examined when other pressures allow.

Oscar Wilde had written in *Lady Windermere's Fan*, in 1892, that a cynic is someone 'who knows the price of everything and the value of nothing'. Edith Wharton takes that further. For Undine Spragg does not even know the price of everything. She is not cynical, just entirely selfish and quite unthinkingly ruthless in the pursuit of what she wants. She does learn during the course of the novel, but not a lot, and then only because it is to her own advantage to learn a few things, like the names of painters who might be worth dropping into conversation.

It is a major achievement on Wharton's part that such an unlikeable character does not irritate the reader to exasperation, as she does her own parents and husbands. But Wharton steers a fine line: she has a gift for making the reader empathize and lose sympathy by turns. She takes the reader inside the minds of her characters, using free direct and indirect speech with wonderful ease, allowing a wide range of perceptions, and enabling the reader's range of sympathy to include even the most unsympathetic of her creations.

Her plotting is masterly, surprising the reader again and again with shifts in time, then predictably bringing back a character (Elmer Moffatt always turns up just when the reader would expect him to) – she moves between surprise and inevitability, to make a plot which is astonishing in its circularity and roundedness. It redresses the balance of the tragic fate of Lily Bart in *The House of Mirth*, but although Undine Spragg's story is no tragedy, its comedy is certainly bitter, savage and hugely ironic.

The very first words of the novel are that name, Undine Spragg. A surprising, explosive opening, and one that fits the character perfectly. It is an outrageous name for an outrageous character. In her introduction to the Penguin Twentieth-Century Classics edition the novelist, Anita Brookner, suggests that the 'name is the only discordant element in a story which is sober, meticulous, and impeccably set forth'. Each reader must decide, but it is precisely that outrageousness which underscores the sobriety of all the rest of the characters. The fact that Undine Spragg's initials are also the initials of her native land is no coincidence. Wharton is brilliant with names, of people and of places. In *The House of Mirth* surely the dreadful aunt, Mrs Peniston, is not named by accident. And in this novel there are many names to rejoice in: the dreadful Indiana Frusk and her fiancé Millard Binch are splendidly named. And there is a touch of strangeness in Elmer Moffatt's name too: it combines the new American and the old world, whereas Peter Van Degen and Ralph Marvell are fully old-style New York names.

The Custom of the Country does not view New York with the nostalgia that would creep into *The Age of Innocence*, written a few years later, after the First World War. Wharton spent the years immediately before and during the war working tirelessly for relief organizations, and for the dispossessed and the war wounded who found themselves in Paris. For this work she was awarded the Légion d'Honneur in 1916. The war, as it did for many of her contemporaries, changed Edith Wharton's perceptions: she began to look back to a golden age before the war, the very age she had so ironically portrayed in *The Custom of the Country*. That could be why there is such a nostalgic tone to the later novel, and might indeed be a major part of that novel's success, where *The Custom of the Country* has received less attention.

Wharton might be describing the last gasp of the *belle époque*, as well as the first floods of what the Goncourt brothers had called as early as the 1860s '*l'américanisation de la France*'. She is describing two societies, each feeding off the other, each remorselessly using the other for its own ends. And at the heart of these societies lies the simple fact of money. Undine Spragg is no more or less than a character who makes her way to the top of these societies. It is a novel about Darwin's principle of the survival of the fittest. It does not go so far as, say, Scott Fitzgerald's *The Great Gatsby* in portraying disillusion: the tone is too robustly ironic for that. Whether Edith Wharton admires or despises her heroine is open to debate. Certainly Undine Spragg crosses over all the borders between respectability and vulgarity. For someone of Wharton's class, divorce was always a rather vulgar concept, even though she herself went through it. There is a pull in all her writing between conservatism and rebellion, between being as strong-willed as Undine undoubtedly is, and 'keeping up appearances', maintaining the old traditions and standards. It is the very unresolved nature of this struggle that gives *The Custom of the Country* its vitality. We still live in a society where the brash and new is in conflict with established ways, where old money and respectability are set against the new iconoclasm. These are eternal clashes in any society. Perhaps the only moment when this novel could have been written was just before the Great War, when ironic comedy was still possible, and when the ceremony of innocence had not yet been drowned, to echo W. B. Yeats's *The Second Coming*.

Some of the customs would change irrevocably after that cataclysm. New customs would make Undine Spragg no less of a heroine for her times, but, as her creator did, the times would invent a different America, a nostalgic America, an innocent America. Edith Wharton's later novels are satires of an America she no longer knew at first hand. She knew the custom of the country when she wrote the novel with that title, and that is what makes it a convincing testament to its times, a novel whose observation, irony and simply brilliant writing make it an immensely enjoyable masterpiece.

The Life and Background of Edith Wharton

The woman who would become world famous as the writer Edith Wharton was born Edith Newbold Jones in New York in 1862. She was born to wealth and social status, and at the age of twenty-three, she married at the proper social level. Her husband Teddy (Edward Robbins Wharton) was twelve years older than she was, and the marriage seems to have lacked passion. There were no children, and by the time Edith wrote *The Custom of the Country* Teddy was suffering from what would now be known as manic depression or bi-polarity. They divorced in 1913.

Edith had been precocious in her creativity as a young girl, but after her marriage she lapsed into silence, only beginning to write very slowly in the 1890s, publishing occasional short stories in magazines until her travels and researches in Europe began to bear fruit.

High Society New Yorkers of the last decades of the nineteenth century, rather like the characters in Henry James's novels, travelled frequently to Europe. Like many in that society the Whartons had no need to work – their income derived from property holdings and inheritance – and as the new leisured class they took to travel and tourism in a big way. Edith was rather less of a dilettante than most of her social equals and contemporaries, however. She researched deeply into architecture, interior design, and Italian art history, and over the years published many books on these subjects. Her first published volume, written in collaboration with the architect Ogden Codman, was *The Decoration of Houses*, a large and well-illustrated book, which went completely against the design tastes of the time in America, and paved the way for new ways of thinking about interior design.

This is one facet of Edith Wharton's personality that can be seen in

The Custom of the Country, where interiors are carefully described, and often reflect negatively on the tastes of the inhabitants of the house (or hotel in Undine's case). But it is not appropriate to seek out Edith Wharton the woman in all her writings, as one of her best biographers, R. W. B. Lewis, is prone to do. He goes so far as to call Undine Spragg in this novel Edith Wharton's 'anti-self'. Her most recent biographer, Shari Benstock, usefully corrects many of the assumptions about her that Lewis perpetuated, and the result is a clearer picture of a dedicated artist, who had no need at all to write for money, but who worked immensely hard, writing every morning when she could, in order to reach her creative expression and fulfilment. She worked in many genres: short stories and novels made her name, but she also wrote a great many travel books (she particularly loved the new opportunities offered by automobile travel); and she wrote plays; translated from French and German; wrote some criticism (*The Writing of Fiction*, for example – although she in general did not review fiction), and in her later years her well-known autobiography *A Backward Glance*. The chronology that follows shows how productive her life was, but one remarkable feature of her autobiography is how little space she devotes to her fiction – one chapter only.

Although it is a mistake to read too much of Edith Wharton's life into her work, there are distinct allusions to her own experience in her novels. The novels of New York Society, beginning with *The House of Mirth* in 1905 and ending with *The Age of Innocence* in 1920 are novels about the society she knew best. The old families and the new money, the rigid social codes, the international travel, the artistic pretensions, the newspaper and magazine gossip columns, the view of divorce as 'scandal' – all of these were familiar to her. She disliked New York intensely every time she went back there. But she did not fall into the trap of holding up France, or Europe in general, as culturally, historically or socially superior. The French society she describes in *The Custom of the Country* is just as stratified, snobbish and open to criticism as American society.

Edith Wharton made her home in France from about 1910, and worked tirelessly for charities and hospitals during the First World War. This she saw as part of her duty as a woman of means: she had the capacity to work for others, rather than just idly to indulge her wealth. In New York she had worked for such charities as the Society for the Protection of Animals. By the time of the war in Europe that age of innocence had passed and her work, which brought her the Légion d'Honneur, was with refugees, the displaced of war and the outcasts of society.

It is wrong to think of Edith Wharton as a rich, isolated matron. From her earliest works onward, critics remarked that she was able to write about lives she could not have experienced, social conditions she had never lived in, and passions which her life would seem not to have contained. That her marriage to Teddy was passionless is assumed, but of course, she would never have betrayed such a secret. What is known is that in her forties she had a lover, William Morton Fullerton; and it would seem that, just as she was at the height of her popular, critical and financial success, she was also at her happiest in her emotional life. This was the time of writing what many consider to be her most ironic and bitter novel, *The Custom of the Country.* And then the Great War intervened, and the age of innocence was past.

Edith Wharton's subject matter in her novels is always twofold – the New York Society she grew up in and came to dislike, and the role of women. Women and how they are perceived both *in* society and *by* society is a constant theme in her work, with the possible exception of her best known and least characteristic story *Ethan Frome*, which was written during the long gestation and writing of *The Custom of the Country.*

Perhaps in *Ethan Frome* she was able to work out the necessity of tragedy, and thereby to keep it out of *The Custom of the Country. The House of Mirth* ends in tragedy for the heroine; *The Custom of the Country* goes beyond tragedy, and ends on a note that is distinctly one of beginning rather than ending, marking it as being without the sense of closure that most novels of her time demanded. In this sense it is fairly unusual, and the ending, the irony (which some critics saw as cynicism) and the sheer selfishness of the heroine all made for an unusually mixed reaction to the novel. It was first published in serial form, as were most of her novels, from January 1913. The serial format gives the chapters pace, generates the possibility of cliff-hanging endings to chapters and creates a sense of suspense which makes the novel highly readable. It also gives Edith Wharton the chance to start the next episode with a time-shift, a surprise, with something that does not follow obviously and directly from the conclusion of the previous episode. She uses this very cleverly to reveal major incidents after they have happened, and to observe the passing of time in ways that prefigure many writers who are considered 'modernist'.

The longer she stayed in Europe, especially after the war, the more distanced she became from American society, and her novels become more obviously satirical, less effective perhaps in their critical observation of that society, which of course was changing very rapidly. In *The Custom of the Country* she catches a moment, a decade in fact, in the development of American society – the first great flush of materialism and of Thorstein Veblen's 'leisure class' (*see* p. **105**). It is a subject which has not dated – indeed it has perhaps become more familiar throughout the intervening years. The phenomenon of rich Americans buying up European cultural artefacts, which is crucial to the final stages of the plot of *The Custom of the Country,* has now become a commonplace. Questions of taste and refinement, of money and art are everywhere in the novel. But the main focus is the selfishness of all the characters: that might be the 'custom' of the new America.

The writing of the novel was not easy for Edith Wharton. She began the novel in Paris as early as the spring of 1908, completing six chapters by July that year, and had hoped to begin serialization in January 1909. She stopped and started work on this novel over the next two or three years, and something of this hesitation can be detected in the more leisurely pace of the early chapters. Apparently it was with the creation of the character of Indiana Frusk in 1911 that the novel began to catch fire, and the writing of most of it was done in 1912 and 1913, just as the divorce from Teddy was in the process of being formalized. She had not completed the story when serialization began in January 1913 in *Scribner's Magazine.* Edith Wharton only finished the final chapters of the novel in early August 1913. The book appeared in volume form in October 1913.

The title, *The Custom of the Country* is an old one, as Edith Wharton was aware. It was the title of a Jacobean play by John Fletcher and

Philip Massinger dating from 1619–1622, where the 'custom of the country' is the *droit de seigneur* of a powerful count. The subject matter of the play is male/female roles and power relationships, but in effect that is all the two works have in common.

Tiny touches of Edith Wharton's own situation might be detected in the novel over and above the divorce theme: the irony of Undine's coming into the money made from the 'deal' with Elmer only after Ralph's death echoes what happened to Edith's own mother, who became independently wealthy only through a coincidental and entirely separate inheritance after the death of her husband, whose death was hastened by money worries in 1882 when Edith Wharton was twenty. And the English actress Undine goes to see in New York could easily refer to a production by Mrs Patrick Campbell's company of a play translated by Edith Wharton herself (Chapter VIII).

But these are precisely the kind of light little touches which serve to show how much the novel is *not* based on Edith Wharton's own experience. Again and again her life story resonates with the kind of characters, names, situations and anomalies that are found in her novels, but it is precisely because they are only hints, allusions, slight touches, that the novels acquire their own quality, related to but quite distinct from the biographical facts of their author's life.

Chronology: Edith Wharton's Life and Works

1859 Charles Darwin: *On the Origin of Species.*
1862 Edith Wharton was born Edith Newbold Jones in New York on 24 January.
1865 End of the American Civil War. Assassination of President Lincoln.
1866–72 The Jones family lives in Europe.
1868 Louisa May Alcott: *Little Women.*
1869 The American West opened up by the Union Pacific railroad and the Standard Oil company.
1870 Death of Charles Dickens.
1876 Mark Twain: *Tom Sawyer.*
1878 Edith Newbold Jones's *Verses* privately published. She was sixteen years old.
1879–83 Introduced to New York Society and travels in France.
1881 Henry James: *Washington Square.*
1882–83 Engaged to be married to Harry Stevens in France (after her father's death and an inheritance of $20,000).
1885 Married (aged twenty-three) to Edward (Teddy) Wharton, a wealthy Bostonian, twelve years her senior.
1888 Cruises the eastern Mediterranean aboard the *Vanadis.*
1891–93 Buys property on Park Avenue, New York City, and Land's End, Newport, Rhode Island.
1897 *The Decoration of Houses* (with Ogden Codman).
1898 Emile Zola: *J'Accuse*, about the Dreyfus case. Zola convicted of libelling the French government.
1899 *The Greater Inclination,* Edith Wharton's first collection of short stories.

Thorstein Veblen: *The Theory of the Leisure Class.*
Second trial and conviction of Alfred Dreyfus for treason. (The first was in 1894.)

1901–03 Becomes wealthy on her mother's death. Plans, and moves into 'The Mount' in Lenox, Massachusetts. Publishes *Crucial Instances* (stories, 1901) and the historical novel *The Valley of Decision* (1902), set in Italy. Teddy Wharton suffers a nervous breakdown. Travels in Europe culminate in buying a Paris apartment in 1907.

1902 Henry James: *The Wings of the Dove.*
Translates the play *Es Lebe das Leben* by Hermann Sudermann, as *The Joy of Living.*

1903 Henry James: *The Ambassadors.*
First meets James in London: the start of a close literary friendship.

1904 *The Descent of Man* (stories) and *Italian Villas and Their Gardens.*

1905 *The House of Mirth* (serialized from January, published in October) is a huge success. Life alternates between The Mount and Paris.

1907 Novella *Madame de Treymes* (which anticipates some of the themes of *The Custom of the Country*) and *The Fruit of the Tree.*

1908 *A Motor-Flight Through France.*

1910 Leaves her husband in Paris; she has had affairs, and Teddy has embezzled some of her money. Publishes *Tales of Men and Ghosts.*
E. M. Forster: *Howards End.*

1911 *Ethan Frome.*
D. H. Lawrence's first novel, *The White Peacock.*

1912 Worsening relations with Teddy Wharton. Publishes *The Reef* (novel).
In this year, *Death in Venice* (Thomas Mann) published in Germany; *Le Grand Meaulnes* (Henri Alain-Fournier) in France.
Sinking of the *Titanic* in the North Atlantic.

1913 *The Custom of the Country.*
Divorces Teddy, travels to Sicily and Germany, and pays a visit to the USA.

1914–18 The First World War. She is closely involved in front-line relief efforts in France, and awarded the Légion d'Honneur in 1916. Writes *Fighting France, from Dunkerque to Belfort* (1915), and edits *The Book of the Homeless* (1916). Meets André Gide in 1915, when both are in their mid-fifties.

1919 André Gide: *La Symphonie Pastorale*.
Edith Wharton rents a château at Hyères (in the département du Var, overlooking the Mediterranean) which she later buys.
Publishes *French Ways and Their Meaning*.

1920 *The Age of Innocence*. This was hugely successful, winning the Pulitzer Prize in 1921, but Edith Wharton's novella *The Old Maid* failed to find a publisher in the same year, as it discusses birth outside marriage.

1922 *The Glimpses of the Moon*.
Also published in this extraordinary year: T. S. Eliot, *The Waste Land*; James Joyce, *Ulysses*; Virginia Woolf, *Jacob's Room*; Sinclair Lewis, *Babbitt*.

1923 Edith Wharton was the first woman to be awarded an Honorary Doctor of Letters degree at Yale University.

later 1920s After the age of sixty (1922), Edith Wharton's literary output has largely been neglected. Her successes pre-dated talking pictures (1928), the Wall Street Crash (1929), and the rise of Hitler in Germany (from 1933).
Four novellas collected (1924) under the title *Old New York*. Her novels from this decade are *The Mother's Recompense* (1925) and *Hudson River Bracketed* (1929), which returns less successfully to the contrast of old New York and new mid-Western values. In 1925, she publishes *The Writing of Fiction*, a work of criticism for which she read widely in modern literature.

1927 Candidate for the Nobel Prize for Literature.

1929 Awarded a Gold Medal by the American Academy of Arts and Letters.
Publication in England of Virginia Woolf's *A Room of One's Own*, and in the USA of William Faulkner's *The Sound and the Fury*.

1930s Continues to publish short stories, *Human Nature* (1933), and

Ghosts (1937), and her autobiography *A Backward Glance* in 1934. She wrote until the year of her death.

1937 Edith Newbold Jones Wharton died on 11 August, from a stroke, aged seventy-five. Buried at Versailles.

The Plot

The plot of the novel is quite simple: it is the character relations and the time-frame which are complex. Details of plot and individual characters are given in the Focus and Follow-Up sections of the Commentary.

Outline of the Plot

Undine Spragg and her parents have come to New York from Apex, where her father made his fortune. In Apex he had carried out some business deals which set the tone for the novel: shady deals and questionable practices abound both there and in Wall Street.

Undine is socially ambitious and makes her way into New York Society, getting her father to provide the money. She marries Ralph Marvell, who belongs to an old family of the leisure class and they travel to Europe, where her horizons begin to expand. They have a son, Paul, but Undine's ambitions now go beyond Ralph, who has had to take a job, and is having financial problems maintaining his wife's expensive lifestyle.

Undine is attracted to Peter Van Degen, whose social status in New York is higher than Ralph's, but although she follows him to Paris and stays with him for two months while not divorced from Ralph, he is shocked by her callous behaviour towards her husband and will not divorce his own wife, Clare. Undine expects Peter Van Degen to follow her to Dakota, where she stays six months, obtaining her divorce from Ralph, and staying with Mabel Lipscomb, who is divorcing her husband Harry.

Ralph hears the truth about Undine's past in Apex and is driven to suicide. Undine, now a widow rather than a divorcée, can marry Raymond de Chelles, who belongs to an old French family which would not earlier seek a papal annulment of her marriage. Again financial constraints become a problem, and the couple follow their separate interests.

Elmer Moffatt, also from Apex, has followed Undine's career very closely, helping Ralph out with a financial deal, and he eventually also brings an ironic form of financial help to Raymond de Chelles when his brother's American father-in-law loses his fortune.

It emerges that part of what went on in Apex before the Spraggs came to New York was that Undine and Elmer were briefly married and divorced. As her marriage to Raymond falls apart, she and Elmer resume their closeness. Despite some financial ups and downs, Elmer becomes a multimillionaire. At the end of the novel, Undine's son Paul Marvell, now almost nine, is seen as an observer of his mother's continuing social climb as Mrs Elmer Moffatt, but with the 'tiny dark cloud' that as a divorced woman she could never become an ambassador's wife.

Time-Frame

The novel opens in New York two years *after* several of the crucial events have taken place in Apex. It ends more or less at the time of its writing, 1912–13. By then it is two years since Undine's remarriage to Elmer Moffatt, and Paul Marvell, her son, is nearly nine years old.

Coincidentally, when Elmer reveals to Ralph the story of Undine's first marriage (pp. 263–4) it is described as having taken place 'nine years ago last month', and before that Undine had been engaged 'for a year or two' to Millard Binch.

With the precise reference contained in the mention of Sir Arthur Conan Doyle's novel *The Hound of the Baskervilles* in the opening chapter, we can place the start of the novel in 1902 or 1903 – the Sherlock Holmes novel was published in 1902. So the earliest actions referred to in Apex must have taken place about 1899.

The entire action of the plot therefore takes in a period of twelve or thirteen years.

Allusions to Ralph's early life and at least one visit to Europe before he meets Undine are not chronologically significant to the plot.

The age of Paul Marvell, the son of Undine and Ralph, is the most regular and precise indicator of the passing of time. He is two years old in Chapter XIV, six in Chapter XXXI, and nearly nine in Chapter XLVI.

Commentary

Note

The novel is in five books and forty-six chapters, which are numbered in Roman numerals I to XLVI

BOOK ONE

Chapter I, *pp. 5–13*

Focus

The opening exclamation of Undine's name by her mother, immediately creates some uncertainty. What is she wailing about? Why should she 'defend' the note? The question might also come to the reader's mind, why are they in a hotel?

The rest of the chapter will establish several things: the atmosphere of snobbery and social levels, differences between Mrs Spragg and her daughter and Mrs Heeny; and the imagery of twisting movement which surrounds Undine, and which might be seen as tying in with the water-sprite implications of her name (*see* Characters p. 93).

Mrs Spragg and the 'stout professional-looking person' Mrs Heeny are both quickly established. The words describing Mrs Spragg emphasize feebleness, and her wrinkles. With Mrs Heeny it is the professional aspect which is underlined, thus already bringing out some layers of social difference, which will recur frequently throughout the novel. There will be a constant underlining of the differences between characters who work and characters who do not work.

Undine's loveliness is already established in the first few lines.

The focus of the chapter lies, however, in the contrasts between pretensions and reality, between ambitions and their lack of fulfilment, between laziness and effort. The letter is an invitation to dinner at Mrs Fairford's, which will be the beginning of something for Undine.

Follow-Up

As well as establishing these three characters, the layers of society are hinted at by the mention of Apex City (p. 9, l. 20) and the story of the family's move to New York 'some two years previously'. Time and the movement of time will be important throughout (for the time-frame of the novel *see* p. **21**).

The description of the interior of the Stentorian (p. 5) is a useful contrast with other interior descriptions of various settings throughout the book. The critic Edmund Wilson said Mrs Wharton was 'not only the pioneer, but the poet of interior decoration', so this will be something to note each time it recurs. This rich and rather pretentious suite gives an air of luxury which is belied by the later discussion of money problems and better addresses. Despite all the potential positive elements of the description, the underlying note is one of failure: the Spraggs have failed to achieve social success in New York, and their accommodation is something of a problem. Mrs Heeny's bag of newspaper clippings is immediately seen as the family's access to high society – they can only hear about it at second hand, and then only through this avid collector of clippings; practically third hand, therefore. This, together with the discussion of what constitutes a 'good' address, again emphasizes the layered nature of the New York society to which Undine (rather than her family) aspires.

The other characters mentioned, Mr Popple and the Marvell family, will assume significant roles later in the novel. It will be worth noting the first mention of Ralph Marvell is less than wholly positive. Mabel Lipscomb's role as an intermediary echoes Mrs Heeny's position: there are always other people between the Spraggs and the people they want to be associated with. The first mention of Elmer Moffatt and Mrs Spragg's reaction (pp. 12–13) give early notice of his significance, which will only become clear very slowly during the course of the story.

Language and Style

In the opening page there is an emptiness behind all the positive descriptions. Wharton uses her long sentences well, to move from positive to less than flattering (see ll. 25–31 for example). In effect, Mrs Heeny is described in more positive terms than Mrs Spragg.

The ornamentation and decoration of the hotel suite is contrasted with the emptiness of the characters' lives. Check out the adjectives used: '*highly-varnished*', '*florid*' contrasting with '*pale*', '*puffy*', '*drooping*'. Mrs Heeny is described quite differently, in terms of solidity and reality. Words and phrases like 'ain't in it' (p. 6, l. 42) 'way down there' (p. 7, l. 18), 'swell' (p. 7, l. 22) and 'poky' (p. 7, l. 41) indicate again something of the social level of the speakers – underlining colloquially the differences the narration is exploring.

There is a neat contrast between the narrative and the journalistic style of the newspaper clippings and the use of words like 'natty little dinners' and clichéd phrases like 'gnashing of teeth' (p. 8). The amused comments on the style of the letter are part of what will become an ongoing reflection on language and its registers and uses that will recur throughout the novel. The words 'their rather precipitate departure from Apex' (p. 10, l. 19) open up an air of mystery. Undine's insistence on hotels rather than keeping 'house' will reverberate throughout the novel, especially when the French word *hôtel* comes in.

Notes

Stentorian (p. 5, l. 19): the hotel's name implies loudness, and so perhaps there is the suggestion that it is not an understated sort of place.

Looey (p. 5, l. 19): a misspelling of Louis, giving the first hint of French pretensions in a novel which will turn out to be full of them. Having a 'Looey' suite and a French maid (her name is Céleste) are the family's first steps on the long road towards Frenchification.

The Hound of the Baskervilles (p. 5, ll. 25–6): the Sherlock Holmes mystery story by Sir Arthur Conan Doyle (1902) is almost the only novel actually named by title in this book. Undine will be seen reading a few other novels, usually not of the highest quality, and usually not named. There is no indication that this copy of the mystery novel is actually read – it might just be 'ornament'. It is mentioned again in Chapter IX (p. 69). Its presence does, however, indicate something of the possible time-frame of the novel.

Useful Quotations

'She filled the double role of manipulator and friend.' (p. 6, l. 3) (of Mrs Heeny)

'Poor Mrs Spragg had done her own washing in her youth, but since her rising fortunes had made this occupation unsuitable she had sunk into the relative inertia which the ladies of Apex City regarded as one of the prerogatives of affluence.' (p. 9, ll. 29–32) (of Mrs Spragg)

"The wrong set's like fly-paper: once you're in it you can pull and pull, but you'll never get out of it again." (p. 11, ll. 16–17) (Undine Spragg)

Chapter II, *pp. 13–21*

Focus

The tone of irony increases as Undine's reading (*Boudoir Chat*) and her pretensions and aspirations become clearer. This chapter focuses on her inconsistencies in terms of fashion, then moves back a long way into her past. Memory becomes future aspiration, as she imagines the impression she will make on Mrs Fairford's guests. Narcissism emerges as a clear part of her character.

Follow-Up

The contrast between Undine's present and her past is sharp. 'Her baffled social yearnings' (p. 16, l. 6) are already clear, and are traced all the way back to her childhood. In New York, a similar memory of her mistake with the Austrian riding-master is a serious indication of her emotional vulnerability The role of the Lipscombs in the past and the present shows how much Undine's career depends on her acquaintances from the past and their more recent connections.

Undine's experience of the society she has aspirations to join is portrayed as unsatisfactory ('at first' contrasts with 'but in time' on p. 19);

this is an indication of the constant dissatisfaction that will come to characterize her behaviour.

'Unsuspected social gradations' (p. 19, l. 28) have been hinted at since the beginning of the story, but only now does Undine begin to notice them. The point about how much she is aware of having learned is one that will be made again and again.

The final note of concern about money and how Undine can handle her father is the beginning of a major line of the narrative.

Language and Style

The letter register is taken up again, and again Mrs Heeny's colloquial speech patterns are brought out.

The idea of Undine as 'some fabled creature whose home was in a beam of light' (p. 15, l. 34) is a romantic touch which is immediately brought back to earth with the move into the past. The imagery of twisting and sparkling, established in the previous chapter, is continued (p. 16). There is a move into her own thoughts with free indirect speech on p. 17. This move between narration and the characters' own thoughts will become a major feature of the novel's style.

Notes

The names of the hotels cover a range of pretensions from classical Greek to English Romanticism (Tintern Abbey is the setting of a poem by Wordsworth) and Venice.

'The Problem-Novel' (p. 19, l. 9): the title refers to novels which tackle social problems. Divorce, for example, or unmarried motherhood, might be the themes of this kind of novel in the 1890s and the first decade of the new century.

Magnet (p. 19, l. 25): mistake for magnate.

Useful Quotations

'Undine was fiercely independent and yet passionately imitative.' (p. 14, l. 12)

"Go steady, Undine, and you'll get anywheres." (p. 17, ll. 26–7) (Mrs Heeny)

Chapter III, *pp. 21–5*

Focus

The opening sentence gives the tone of disappointment. The main thrust of the chapter is exclusion: the sense that all the families in New York society are 'more or less cousins'. The other theme is Undine's lack of taste.

Follow-Up

The interior of the house contrasts with the description of the Stentorian suite in Chapter I: the word 'no' is repeated; 'shabby' and 'old' reinforce Undine's feelings. Clearly most of these adjectives are chosen by her – they represent her perception and her judgement of the society she aspires to. The narratorial comment (p. 21, l. 24) that 'Undine was too young to take note of culinary details' is interesting, pointing up a contrast between her own choice of adjectives and the presence of the omniscient narrator. It will be worth observing the movement between how Undine's thoughts are represented and the narrator's own observations.

Several of the new characters encountered will become significant during the novel, and it will be worth noting who they are: Peter Van Degen's wife Clare, Harriet Ray, Mr Popple the artist, and of course 'young Marvell' are particularly important. He is described as 'shy' and 'quiet' on this first meeting. Mrs Van Degen is also described rather negatively at first (p. 24, l. 3ff). However, Undine keeps thinking back to Apex City.

Note how often the word 'but' comes into the description in the paragraph covering pp. 22–3. But Undine changes her opinion of 'Ralphie' by the end – consistency is not her strong point.

The painter and talk of painting will become emblematic of how this society sees itself and wants to be represented. The fact that Mr Popple is described as 'the only gentleman I know' (p. 23, l. 26) is neatly punctured in the next line. In effect, the narrator is questioning the whole nature of what is a 'gentleman' and social status and respectability. 'A Van Degen reason' is similarly pointed. The conversation, in which Undine feels left out, will be a recurring feature all through the novel. She constantly betrays her lack of culture: her 'culture' is low, popular stuff, and 'higher' culture is beyond her.

Language and Style

To begin a chapter with 'though' is indicative: it gives a kind of musical note of negativity to what was expected to be positive. This kind of language-based contrast is something Wharton is particularly good at, and will be found all through the novel, underscoring linguistically the thematic contrasts and emotional conflicts of Undine.

Her conversational abilities are skilfully revealed as pretty empty, so the reader will find her sudden hope to be invited to the opera naïve and revealing of her own lack of self-awareness. The adverb 'stupidly' in the second last line of the chapter is a strong one – is it the narrator, or Undine's own perception of herself?

Notes

Sarah Bernhardt (p. 24, ll. 36–7): Undine gets the name slightly wrong. She was the greatest actress of her time (1845–1923). (She was indeed quite old if Undine saw her in the early 1900s in New York.) The plays whose titles Undine gets wrong too, are *L'Aiglon* (1900) by Edmond Rostand (1868–1918) and *Phèdre* (1677), by Jean Racine (1639–1699).

(In October 1902 Undine would have been able to see the English actress Mrs Patrick Campbell at the Garden Theater, Madison Square Garden, in *The Joy of Living*, translated from a German text by none other than Edith Wharton.)

Useful Quotations

'Married men were intrinsically uninteresting.' (p. 22, l. 14)

'Undine did not even know that there were any pictures to be seen, much less that "people" went to see them.' (p. 24, ll. 26–7)

Chapter IV, *pp. 26–37*

Focus

This chapter broadens the irony: Undine's ambition to go to the opera is not just a whim. It will become a significant point of reference. The narrator's mention of 'national belief in the duty of reciprocal "treatment"' echoes the reference on p. 23 to 'the national note of irony'. The cost of the opera box and Undine's insistence on it tie in with the theme of being 'observed' and noticed, which has its positive and its negative aspects.

Follow-Up

The reader might now begin to be irritated by Undine's demands, and her view of the role of men 'to bring back the spoils to their women' (p. 28, l. 14). Her wish also 'to discipline her mother' (p. 28, l. 28) might alienate some sympathy from Undine herself. This is part of Wharton's careful orchestration of the reader's sympathy throughout the novel.

The trip to the gallery is important for the first encounter with Peter Van Degen. However, she did not notice the paintings and later her novel remains 'unread' on her knee.

The past encounters with people from elsewhere in America will become significant too – Miss Wincher in particular (*see* p. 164). The covering of so much of America is indicative: as the nation grows, Undine's focus becomes more and more limited to New York, despite her 'pioneer' blood. She in effect rejects the rest of America, no matter how 'exclusive', for New York.

The mention of Elmer at the end of the chapter is nicely tantalizing: the reader must now be aware that he is always present somewhere in the background of the story.

Language and Style

There is an increasing examination of Undine's feelings and the verbs like 'fluttered' of Mrs Spragg and 'discipline' of Undine indicate something of the effect Undine is creating on her family. Mr Spragg's identifying 'toothpick' is becoming a noticeable feature of descriptions of him. Money is of course becoming a deeper concern – Undine's attitude becomes clear here, and will change little from here onwards. Her patronizing tone towards Mabel Lipscomb is also worth noting – loyalty to old friends and allies is not part of Undine's character.

Adjectives chosen by the narrator take on an edge: 'arrogant' for example, while Undine's choice of adjectives and other lexis only reinforces her self-obsession: 'an imperfect understanding of what constituted the necessities of life' for example. The story of her past 'struggles' reinforces this edge, and moves the narration back into the past and out of New York, with the digs against the Frusks, and 'the boredom of the Mealey House routine'. It is worth noting how Undine is bored everywhere – phrases like 'the day wore on' have indicated this in New York too.

The word 'afterward' (p. 34, l. 2) is an interesting anticipation of future awareness.

Useful Quotations

'Undine . . . swept . . . out of the door . . ., with scorn and anger in every line of her arrogant young back.' (p. 28, ll. 22–4)

"Father was a rich man for Apex, but that's different from being rich in New York." (p. 29, ll. 19–21)

'What was the use of being beautiful and attracting attention if one were perpetually doomed to relapse again into the obscure mass of the Uninvited?' (p. 31, ll. 38–40)

'From small things to great, everything went against her.' (p. 35, ll. 37–8)

Chapter V, *pp. 37–45*

Focus

This is the opera chapter and is, in some ways, Undine's first success, although of course it is tempered, as all of her successes are. It is full of binaries and contrasts from the very first lines about looking from above or below, and now looking on the same level. Presence/absence, longing/rejection, having and not having are strongly stressed.

Follow-Up

Peter Van Degen and Ralph Marvell begin to take on more significance, although the hints are more towards Peter than Ralph still. As Undine aspires to move socially upwards, she despises more and more those who have helped her, like Mabel.

The discussion of painting and the praise for Undine's hair confirm some of the ideas already seen – Undine's hair always seems to be her best feature.

At p. 43 the narrative moves completely away from Undine and her family for the first time. It is significant therefore that the focus shifts briefly to Ralph; he judges Popple, who effectively damns himself out of his own mouth. The reflections on architecture and the new perspective of the city show something of Ralph's (and the narrator's?) attitudes to the city and its 'social disintegration'.

The mention of 'Aborigines' and 'the invading race' (p. 45) is highly significant in its indications of Washington Square society ('the Reservation'), seen through Ralph Marvell's eyes. It superimposes on the original native American inhabitants of the continent (who are simply never considered) a new race who claim to be the original inhabitants, the old New York families – again a layering of society, but a distinct colonizing occupation, which, taken with the novel's use of the outer reaches of America as frontier territory where anything goes, like divorce, begins to give a picture of how the society of Washington Square considered itself and its role. Ralph comes to be seen as in many ways the epitome of that society, so it is interesting that Wharton allows the reader to share his perceptions of it so early in the story.

Language and Style

The words Undine chooses to describe 'them' from the outset indicate that most of this chapter is seen through her eyes. She is also judging Mabel, and again the adjectives she chooses are revealing: 'planted, blonde and brimming' (p. 39, ll. 8–9) are just the beginning. This culminates in the judgement that Mabel is 'ridiculous' (p. 40, ll. 9–10).

In the final part of the chapter the shift of perceptions to Ralph is striking: where the reader has been close to Undine all the way through, there is now a completely different perspective – from within the society that Undine aspires to. Ralph's critical observations of it seem negative at first, but effectively conclude with a statement of high conservatism, which might be seen as complacency: 'They're right' he repeats (p. 44, l. 17).

Useful Quotations

'It was precisely at this moment that there dawned on Undine what was to be one of the guiding principles of her career: "*It's better to watch than to ask questions.*"' (p. 40, ll. 18–21)

'. . . society was really just like the houses it lived in: a muddle of misapplied ornament over a thin steel shell of utility.' (p. 44, ll. 30–31) (Ralph Marvell)

'. . . the ideals of aboriginal New York . . . were singularly coherent and respectable as contrasted with the chaos of indiscriminate appetites which made up its modern tendencies.' (p. 45, ll. 7–10) (Ralph Marvell)

Chapter VI, *pp. 45–50*

Focus

This chapter does with Ralph what has earlier been done with Undine – tracing his memories. These are of course a total contrast with Undine's: Harvard and Oxford, premier universities in Massachusetts and in England, are more than geographically distant from Apex City. The focus on Ralph begins to show how important he will become in the novel.

Ralph is not spared narratorial ironic comments, however: 'this desultory dabbling with life' is the beginning of a growing tone of criticism of Ralph's lack of awareness of the real modern world. 'Social faith' and the customs of the tribe might be the theme of the chapter.

Follow-Up

Ralph's 'inner world' does not get much sympathy either, although it does allow the reader to empathize with him in some ways. His secret cave of childhood is not unlike Edith Wharton's own claim that her writing was her 'secret garden'. His wanting 'to learn and to do' are to be seen as positive aspects of his character, but his intellectual dabbling is made fun of.

Harriet Ray, not an important character in the novel, is, however, a significant presence at the heart of Washington Square – it is worth noticing that she 'was determined, if she married, never to receive a divorced woman' (p. 47, ll. 24–5). This is an early sounding of what will become a very important note.

The contrast between Ralph's lack of a profession and the high comedy of Mrs Spragg's garrulous narration of the naming of Undine after a hair-waver and her father's career in Apex ('he was educated for an undertaker') is one of the finest juxtapositions in the book. The irony is shared almost equally between the two, who are both to be, in their different ways, victims of Undine. This comic telling of part of the past of the Spragg family is a nice contrast with other treatments of the past, through Undine's own eyes, for example.

The final paragraphs suggest Ralph is falling in love with Undine: he sees himself as some kind of romantic rescuer of her, with her as a sacrificial victim to Society.

Language and Style

'Unfinished' might be the key to how things around Ralph are described: all the language promises but never actually delivers, and this neatly sums up his character, right from the beginning – the lists, the accumulated phrases, all seem to be building to something, but simply gather, never arriving at anything much. The pace is slower than the nervous, restless pace of the descriptions of Undine and her wants. The contrast between the two characters is not yet explicit, but is already suggested in the language, the phrases, the sense of complacent incompleteness. His mingling with 'the Invaders' is notable for its comment on language: 'they spoke the same language as his, though on their lips it had often so different a meaning' (p. 47, ll. 38–9). This continues the observation of language and idiom that was noted in the speech patterns of Mrs Heeny, and will come up again and again.

Mrs Spragg's telling of her story brings in another style of reported speech, after 'the first touch on the weak springs of her garrulity' (p. 48, l. 7).

Ralph then moves on to judging people, much as he judged his own society earlier. His thoughts are full of questions and exclamation marks – the variations of punctuation are another of Wharton's stylistic devices. It is no accident that the last paragraph, representing Ralph's thoughts, is unfinished.

Notes

diverse et ondoyant (p. 48, l. 14; p. 50, l. 14): from Montaigne, *Essais*.

Undine's name (p. 48, l. 19): *see* p. 93. '*Un*doolay' = *onduler*, to curl; wavy (of hair) would be *ondoyant*; (to crimp would be *friser*).

Andromeda (p. 50, l. 26): Greek mythical heroine, who was chained to a rock as a sacrifice and rescued by Perseus, whom she married.

Pegasus (p. 50, l. 28): mythical Greek winged horse.

Rosinante (p. 50, l. 29): the (earth-bound) horse of Don Quixote in Cervantes' novel (1605).

Useful Quotations

'His profession was the least real thing in his life.' (p. 45, ll. 21–2) (Ralph Marvell)

'"like a gentleman" – that is with a tranquil disdain for mere money-making.' (p. 45, ll. 32–3) (Ralph Marvell)

'That was long ago, as time is reckoned under thirty.' (p. 46, ll. 27–8)

'Harriet Ray was neither vulgar nor ambitious. She regarded Washington Square as the birthplace of Society.' (p. 47, ll. 20–22)

Chapter VII, *pp. 50–57*

Focus

Mrs Heeny's colloquialisms and Undine's ring take the reader directly into the contrasts the story so far has set up. The first meeting with 'the old man' (old Mr Dagonet, Ralph's grandfather) is daunting, but turns out to be less 'formidable' than she expected. (However, it will be referred to much later.) The mention of divorce towards the end of the chapter is shocking, and a premonition of things to come. It is interesting how words like 'love' are avoided, and 'engagement' is only used in terms of the ring. Spoken/unspoken becomes a binary here. The innocent mention of any possible previous engagement is a case in point (*see* p. 67).

Undine is now at the level that she can read about herself in the newspapers that Mrs Heeny reads: as if the life she leads is not real until it is reported and read about.

Follow-Up

The opening dialogue is something of a return to the opening chapter, and the dinner party also contains echoes of the Fairford dinner in Chapter III. So, although the plot is moving forward in time, Edith Wharton cleverly keeps the past in sight. Clearly one of the less stated parts of the story is the hint of opposition to the marriage from Mrs Marvell. But the whole chapter is moving forward to the fateful mention of divorce, and the ambivalent judgement of Mr Dagonet on Undine.

Language and Style

The narrative skips forward two months here, and looks straight at the ring. This is the first of such leaps in time, which will become a familiar feature in the later books of the novel. There is a great contrast between the opening dialogue and the dinner party, underlining the social layers and differences. Again Undine's conversational inadequacy is stressed, in long flowing sentences which ironically belie the silence and inadequacy they describe.

When describing the older members of society such as old Mr Dagonet, Edith Wharton seems to resort to an older-fashioned style, using these longer sentences, which might appropriately be seen as reminiscent of Henry James.

The talk of divorce is neatly associated with Apex – it is not part of Washington Square society – and Undine underlines her difference from her hosts with this gaffe. Note the verb to 'go round' – it is a serious occupation in this society. The old man assumes the divorce is because the man has been 'misbehaving himself' – the assumption is that it has nothing to do with the woman's wishes.

Notes

Signers (p. 54, l. 4): the men who signed the American Declaration of Independence.

Useful Quotations

'Undine found herself astray in a new labyrinth of social distinctions.' (p. 56, ll. 18–19)

Chapter VIII, *pp. 57–63*

Focus

Tension is avoided by the move to the theatre. Mrs Fairford's gift of control and people management is quietly stressed. But Undine wants to 'get even' for the night at the opera. She enjoys being admired, anonymously and by society names.

The arrangements with the artist Popple sound promising, but her triumph is blighted by the encounter with her unnamed neighbour.

Follow-Up

There are already signs of resentment in Undine, even in the moment of her triumph (p. 60, l. 10). This happens just before her full awareness of her neighbour, who turns out to be Elmer Moffatt: a carefully orchestrated encounter, which shows the thoroughness of Wharton's plotting. Of course he is simply a presence at first (p. 58), but it is significant that it is 'a large imitation pearl' that is the first real sign she notices, and significant also that Apex is mentioned twice in the two pages before the encounter.

She rejects him, but agrees to see him and he gives her his address, ironically in the Driscoll building.

Language and Style

The dialogue between Undine and her unnamed neighbour is a very neat creation of mystery: the reader has to be intrigued by someone from her past whom she does not want to talk to now. It is the first time Undine has been at a real loss as to how to behave. The man's attitude is both surprised and discreet, and the words he uses like 'bargain', and the concision with which he gives the address, indicate something precise and business-like about his character, even though it is not yet clear who he is.

Then the mention of Harmon Driscoll and the Eubaw Mine (p. 61, l. 34) brings the business world fully in to the leisured scene: Clare's evaluation of him is very positive. She is aware of the kinds of advantage he might bring. (It will be worth noting when the Driscoll name recurs, as it becomes important in the very last chapter. *See also* p. 66.)

The return to her own home, where the day started at the beginning of the previous chapter, underlines the difference between her family and society. Here she is called Undie; and her mother seems to intuit what has happened to her, although the reader is still not sure who he was.

Notes

toilets (p. 58, l. 35): costumes (also on p. 288).

Useful Quotations

'It was characteristic of her that she remembered her failures as keenly as her triumphs.' (p. 58, l. 39–41)

Chapter IX, *pp. 63–70*

Focus

This is the meeting in the Park with Elmer, and the first major revelation of Undine's past as what yet another newspaper, *The Apex Eagle*, called in its headlines 'The Child-bride' (p. 65, l. 38); Undine is disturbed and does not want to meet Ralph, so she clearly has a lot to hide – the air of mystery is deepening. Her engagement to Millard Binch is revealed, but, of course, the revelations are only partial for the moment.

Follow-Up

There is a sense of complicity throughout the conversation, culminating in Elmer's asking Undine for help after her marriage. He is just as ambitious socially as she is.

On her return home the deliberate reference to *The Hound of the Baskervilles* very clearly refers back to the opening chapter, which took place almost three months before, so it would be more remarkable if it was still the same novel that was on the onyx table. But the mention serves to emphasize one major difference: that Ralph is now in that very suite. Their conversation is quite different in atmosphere from the one with Elmer – it is tense, and they are pulling in different directions, even though it is he who comes up with the idea of marrying sooner rather than later. Her agreement is not out of love, but out of her desire to escape to Europe.

Language and Style

The language of the conversation about the shared past is deliberately vague and allusive: 'our little unpleasantness at Apex' (p. 66, l. 26) is almost a cliché now. How Elmer has managed to turn this to his advantage is an important part of his character throughout the novel, and one of the key thematic uses Wharton makes of binaries and reversals of fortune.

The mention of 'Uncle' (p. 66, l. 23) in relation to Driscoll is not taken up again.

'. . . it was good while it lasted, wasn't it?' (p. 66, l. 40) might be seen as hinting at more than has been stated. Looking back with knowledge of what happens later in the novel it becomes a highly significant positive line.

The words and the silences between Undine and Ralph are quite different in their tensions and unstated thoughts from the earlier conversation in the Park.

Notes

bewfay (p. 67, l. 34): Elmer's pronunciation of 'buffet'.

Lohengrin (p. 68, l. 20): opera (1850) by Richard Wagner

(1813–1883), which is known for the famous Wedding March. Ironic that Elmer should use it here with Undine!

Useful Quotations

'Nevertheless something in his look seemed to promise the capacity to develop into any character he might care to assume.' (p. 64, ll. 20–21) (of Elmer Moffatt)

Chapter X, *pp. 70–80*

Focus

As the story moves towards marriage, the question of business and a profession becomes more significant: the two themes are inextricably related. Two weeks have passed since the previous chapter, and one week remains before the marriage.

The opening paragraph shows how Mr Spragg is 'another man' in business: home and office become a binary. The conversation with Mr Dagonet is indicative of many things: his power and his awareness of Ralph's limitations, and the financial burden on Mr Spragg. Undine's refusal to consider any other option is a decisive exercise of her power.

Follow-Up

'The right people' (p. 73, l. 8) are clearly more important than love, which gets a very rare mention (p. 73, l. 21). Marriage and money begin to link in with such names as Representative Rolliver, and of course the ever-present Elmer, who now seems to pose a threat, if he talks (p. 74, l. 27).

What should be a climax, the marriage of Undine and Ralph, is not actually described – Book One ends in an office, and the discussions are largely financial.

Language and Style

There is a lot of sympathy generated for Mr Spragg: 'I'll see what I can do' is picked up immediately in 'he had been "seeing" now for an arduous fortnight' (p. 74, l. 40). The narrator's choice of adjective reinforces the endless connection between marriage and money.

The reappearance of Elmer, with hindsight, is highly appropriate, and his 'I don't want to forbid the banns' (p. 77, ll. 13–14) means more than the reader might catch at first – he could effectively stop the wedding, but does not. Instead he proposes a politically connected deal with Mr Spragg, a sign of his business drive, and the bringing together of past and present, towards the future. Elmer's brief confrontation with Ralph takes on a note of irony: while Ralph has ordered a necklace for Undine, Elmer is talking much more serious business. Whatever the case, it is Mr Spragg who has to pay.

Useful Quotations

'A New York marriage involved material obligations unknown to Apex.' (p. 71, ll. 4–5)

"Nobody expects to make money in a *profession*." (p. 71, l. 23)

BOOK TWO

Chapter XI, *pp. 81–90*

Focus

This is the honeymoon chapter, with idyllic pictures of Italy in summer. But of course there are strong hints that despite all the claimed perfection, there are difficulties. The 'antique land' (p. 87, ll. 19–20) is a quotation from Shelley's sonnet 'Ozymandias', an indication of the contrast between ancient Europe and new America. Undine comments that 'all these places seem as if they were dead. It's all like some awful cemetery' (p. 89, ll. 29–30).

Follow-Up

Again there has been a time shift: four months have passed (p. 81, l. 16).

The mention of the Count Roviano might arouse some suspicion in the reader's mind. However, he is not a problem: the tensions are between Undine and Ralph; but Ralph will look back on this as the high point of his marriage (*see* p. 127), already seeing the signs of

Undine's restlessness. This is also the moment for reflections on inspiration and the meaning of life (p. 89, ll. 7–8). The whole chapter is something of an interlude in the progress of the story, although it contains all the fluctuations between positive and negative that characterize the entire plot. It gives the narrator the opportunity (p. 86) to examine the limited range of Undine's horizons and 'the narrow compass of her experience'. This is more direct criticism than ironic comment and, although filtered through Ralph's perceptions, it begins to build a serious case against Undine – marriage has not actually changed or improved her, as readers might have hoped the achievement of her social aims might do.

Language and Style

The atmosphere of sunshine and languid enjoyment is a total contrast from the America of Book One. It is almost the ideal of the American view of Italy, but from the opening lines there is also the negative power of the heat, despite the beauty and the relaxed atmosphere. The heat becomes one of Undine's excuses for moving on, but the narrator does point out that 'she was sick to death of being alone with him' (p. 85, ll. 25–6).

This is one of the few moments in the novel where the world of nature is given prominence: the usual setting is cities, and later the St Désert scenes (Book Five) are almost a total contrast in terms of nature with the settings here.

Again the word 'afterward' (p. 84, l. 13) looks forward to a time when things are perceived differently. Ralph is already aware of something wrong in the relationship: 'renewed communion with his problems' (p. 87, l. 15) and the constant pressures of money that beset him even in the midst of a perfect setting.

Notes

the Engadine (p. 85, l. 6): the valleys of the River Inn in Switzerland, where St Moritz is situated. Undine will return here with Elmer (p. 325).

Sheban (p. 87, l. 5): reference to the wealth and extravagance of the biblical Queen of Sheba.

Prometheus (p. 88, l. 41): Greek hero, who stole fire from heaven, and was punished by being chained to a rock, where his liver was constantly eaten by a vulture.

Useful Quotations

'. . . her variations on the eternal feminine still enchanted him.' (p. 84, l. 41)

'. . . with a vague clutch at some solution which should keep him a little longer hanging half-way down the steep of disenchantment.' (p. 87, ll. 31–3)

Chapter XII, *pp. 90–100*

Focus

With the couple still journeying, the sense of an interlude, now in Switzerland, continues; when they reach Paris, the second main setting of the novel, the interlude will be over. In Switzerland the reappearance of Roviano, the cavalry officer from Siena, might be a negative note. But there is still, at least in Ralph, a sense also of hope, the hope of 'recapturing the moonlight vision' of the previous chapter (p. 92, ll. 8–9). It is worth noticing that yet again Ralph's sentence is unfinished. Undine's ambitions, after only five months of marriage, have already gone far beyond Ralph, and he is struck by her 'tenacity' in getting what she wants (p. 96, l. 35).

Follow-Up

With all these titled people around, Ralph feels the 'first twinge of jealousy' (p. 92, l. 31), and although the novel is not about jealousy, this is an interesting reflection: the kind of company Undine is now beginning to seek out anticipates the very last chapter of the novel in many ways. She does not want to understand the rules and conventions of this society, however, meaning to follow her own (p. 94, ll. 4–11). This will be developed later as a theme.

The financial difficulties of her father and her claim for help from Ralph's sister Laura are indications of things to come. The presence of Peter Van Degen begins to become slightly ominous: 'you're not over the honeymoon yet' (p. 98, ll. 25–6). He sets up Ralph's relationship with Clare, as well as his own with Undine.

Language and Style

Ralph's past is briefly glimpsed in his very negative judgement of the people they are now encountering (p. 92, para. 2), and the adjectives used are a significant contrast with the ideal world, already lost, of the previous chapter. References to Ralph's work and the lexical choices that bring out his romantic idealistic nature are understated when compared with Undine's social climbing, but they are a useful insight into his character, and are perhaps the first signs that he is not among the category of the 'fittest' to survive in this world.

Later he begins to see her eyes as 'the eyes of an enemy' (p. 96, ll. 5–6).

Useful Quotations

'. . . what strange specimens from the depths slip through the wide meshes of the watering-place world.' (p. 92, ll. 22–3)

Chapter XIII, *pp. 100–108*

Focus

Peter Van Degen begins to assume more importance, and this chapter shows Ralph's judgements on him, and on the society to which Undine now aspires. He sees Van Degen as 'a bore in society and an insufferable nuisance on closer terms' (p. 100, ll. 31–2), a judgement which will take on stronger resonances as the plot progresses. Plans for the return voyage on Van Degen's *Sorceress* give Ralph the chance to assert his authority.

The financial concerns continue with Undine's taste for shopping, and the announcement of her pregnancy at the end of the chapter, which might be expected to be positive, is played out in tears and recriminations.

Follow-Up

The gradations of Ralph's feelings for Undine are marked; he is all the way to disgust already. He learns very quickly, but still cares enough to want to do the best for her. And when he realizes she is pregnant, he goes right back to where he started.

Language and Style

It is very significant how the bald statement of Ralph's disgust, 'Undine was no longer beautiful' (p. 102, l. 40) is unmodified, and in a sense unprepared for, like a sudden realization. It should surprise the reader, given his romantic vocabulary up till now. He realizes too that hopes of 'saving her from Van Degenism' were only 'old dreams' (p. 103, l. 6).

The thought of her pregnancy takes Ralph back, however, to idealistic notions: 'the woman a man loves is always a special case'. This is a rare instance of the use of the word 'love' (p. 106, l. 24).

Useful Quotations

'. . . the only road to her reason lay through her vanity.' (p. 103, ll. 24–5)

Chapter XIV, *pp. 108–17*

Focus

This is the chapter about art, and Mr Claud Walsingham Popple is the target of a considerable amount of narratorial irony. In fact, this is perhaps the novel's central chapter of irony about the pretensions of New York society, art and life, old families and new money.

There has been a surprising time shift, indicated in Popple's perception: 'four years after' (p. 108, l. 36) his first meeting with Undine. The reader might justifiably feel a little confused (*see* p. 21 for the time-frame of the novel), especially since Undine is now revealed as having a press-agent and a son, in that order. Later she will forget the boy's birthday, taken up as she is with her discussions with Peter Van Degen, and the questions, yet again, of accommodation and money.

Follow-Up

Popple 'always subordinated art to elegance' (p. 108, l. 21). His art is 'the essence of good breeding' (p. 108, l. 30). The sense of decorum this implies goes deeply into all aspects of the society he paints, and can be read as indicating very much what Edith Wharton in the novel does *not* want her art to represent. Clearly it is not in Popple's commercial interest to portray any blemishes in his sitters – he paints society as society wants to see itself and this flattery gets him everywhere. Vanity is a key word here: 'idealizing flesh and realizing dress-fabrics' (p. 112, l. 34), and it sums up his achievement.

What is forgotten in all this social pretension is Undine's son, and his birthday. The personal has been sacrificed for the public.

Language and Style

The narrator is bitingly satirical about Popple's 'rhetoric' and his literary tastes as well. The Fifth Reader (p. 110, l. 26) is a school textbook – his intellectual reach does not go beyond that. And that is quite enough to flatter Undine's intellectual pretensions. So his 'mastery' in the discussion of the modern novel is as hollow as the kinds of book he mentions, which are 'served up' in a 'disguise' that cheapens both history and literature (p. 110, l. 29).

That this discussion leads on to Peter Van Degen and the contrast between old families and new millionaires is no accident. And Undine's vanity is at the heart of all of this (p. 111, para. 4).

Only after this, does the narration refer to Undine's 'return to New York' and the feeling that she had made a mistake in her marriage. Society is more important, and the group that now comes to view the painting is depicted as superficial: a nice range of adjectives being used to describe them individually (p. 112, para. 3), and culminating in the judgement 'not one of the number was troubled by any personal theory of art' (p. 112, ll. 30–31).

Elmer Moffatt is not allowed to disappear from the reader's memory, however, as the Driscoll question (cf. pp. 76–9) and the Ararat Trust investigation begin to impinge on the characters' awareness. The presence of Jim Driscoll at Popple's studio and his wife Mamie's comment on the necessary size of the proposed painting

(p. 113, l. 16–17) are an ironic prefiguring of their presence in the very final pages of the novel.

Notes

chafing-dish (p. 108, l. 35): a dish for cooking at the dining-table. The idea is that the behind-the-scenes preparations are never seen, there are no 'messy' elements in the art.

dress him in stripes (p. 113, l. 37): send him to prison. Elmer's relationship with the Driscoll family here and in the final pages of the novel is another example of Wharton's careful plotting.

swinging on a strap in the elevated (p. 116, l. 11): Ralph is commuting on public transport, the elevated railway, in contrast with Peter Van Degen's automobile.

Useful Quotations

". . . *he* knows how we live and what we want." (p. 113, ll. 4–5) (Peter Van Degen, about Popple)

"Oh, hang waiting for the bill – won't a couple of thou' make it all right?" (p. 117, ll. 8–9) (Van Degen to Undine)

Chapter XV, *pp. 117–27*

Focus

The consequences of Undine's forgetting her son's birthday culminate in her first major lie to Ralph and his realization of it, and suspicion about the relationship with Peter Van Degen. It is significant that it is Mrs Fairford (Laura) who first comments on her repeated breaking of engagements: throughout the novel she is perhaps the New York character who behaves best, whatever the circumstances. Both the dialogue between Laura and Charles and Ralph's distress at what has happened swing sympathy decidedly towards him and away from Undine.

In many ways this chapter might be seen as the emotional heart of the novel, and the turning-point in the marriage of Undine and Ralph.

Follow-Up

The reader learns that Ralph 'has had to go into business' (p. 118, ll. 17–18). This pointedly recalls the conversation between Mr Dagonet and Mr Spragg in Chapter X (which is also where Driscoll had been mentioned earlier).

Laura and Charles Bowen discuss American marriages quite cynically. Bowen's remark that 'the average American looks down on his wife' (p. 118, ll. 38–9) gets a strong reaction from Laura. Actually it is not altogether appropriate to Ralph and Undine's marriage, hence perhaps Laura's use of the word 'paradox' in response. The difference between European women 'in the very middle of the picture' and the role of the American wife is significant in the novel's examination of American ways of pretending 'to themselves and each other that *that's* what really constitutes life!' (p. 120, ll. 11–12). Taken with the previous chapter, this dialogue is highly meaningful in the overall vision of the novel's themes.

Language and Style

The fact that the serious themes of relationships, American-ness, social differences between America and Europe, and even divorce are treated in an extended dialogue between two of the less important characters in the novel is interesting. Wharton does not usually give her characters the opportunity for such long and serious discussions, as the frivolity of the previous chapter underlines. It is worth noting also that men and women are criticized equally here: it is not a discussion of Undine and Ralph's marriage as such, but is more a general discussion of American manners and modes.

The smoothness with which the conversation moves on to 'the key to our easy divorces' (p. 120, l. 2) is almost the story of the novel in miniature (and in theory only, of course). The reader is not necessarily asked to agree or sympathize, but the next step, declaring that 'it's Ralph who's the victim and the exception' (p. 120, ll. 23) is perhaps not expected.

Ralph's arrival breaks up the dialogue, and his reactions are a fine example of dramatic irony, setting him up for the full realization that the relationship has now moved beyond 'the ever-renewed dread of small daily deceptions, evasions, subterfuges' (p. 123, ll. 5–6). He goes back in his mind to the early stages of the relationship, after the birth of the boy. However, the usual pattern of the positive being quickly balanced out by the negative soon reasserts itself and reaches a decisive point at 'the discovery that she was completely unconscious of states of feeling on which so much of his inner life depended marked a new stage in their relation' (p. 123, ll. 39–41). This is very fine emotional writing, sensitive and not the least self-indulgent in its portrayal of Ralph's feelings and responses.

His reflections move between narration and free indirect thought, and it is worth noticing that the closeness to Clare now begins to emerge, and he sees this in a rather tribal way: 'after all he and she were of the same blood and had the same traditions' (p. 124, ll. 4–5). But it is Clare (p. 124) who brings up the name (and mystery) of Elmer Moffatt and the night at the theatre. (*See* pp. 60–61 where Clare actually said, 'If he has anything to do with the Driscolls you'd better cultivate him,' words which now can be read with more significance.)

After Undine's return, what is not said between Ralph and his wife becomes as significant as anything that has been said.

Perhaps the resetting of the ring and pendant can be read as symbolic of the relationship: Undine transforming what is old and precious to her own tastes, and then asking for her whim to be paid for.

Useful Quotations

". . . the passion for making money has preceded the knowing how to spend it." (p. 119, ll. 22–3) (Charles Bowen)

". . . money and motors and clothes are simply the big bribe she's paid for keeping out of some man's way." (p. 120, ll. 16–17) (Charles Bowen)

'The flame of love that had played about his passion for his wife had died down to its embers.' (p. 125, ll. 27–28) (Ralph Marvell)

'. . . suddenly, as they stood there face to face, almost touching, she became something immeasurably alien and far off.' (p. 127, l. 20) (Ralph Marvell)

Chapter XVI, *pp. 127–135*

Focus

Ralph's memories, especially of the perfect idyll of the honeymoon (pp. 81–4) are introduced with a brief paragraph that is worthy of George Eliot. It is highly significant that the omniscient narrator avoids the use of any personal pronouns, even a generalized 'we' here (which Eliot might well have done). It is a simple observation rather than a moral point that is being made.

Ralph's reflections use the image of reading between the lines, of 'surface-language' (p. 127, l. 35). He follows his thoughts through illusion to the 'joyless solace' (p. 128, l. 41) of being able to see things impartially. He has even gone beyond suspicion of her relationship with Peter Van Degen.

Follow-Up

Ralph's reflections lead inexorably to money, and more unfinished sentences. Elmer Moffatt is seen as having lost (a rare occurrence), and Van Degen is clearly in the ascendant. Wharton is always careful in her balance of the male characters in Undine's life. The balance between America and Europe also begins to be more significant here with Peter Van Degen's departure. Her realization that he is 'still the stronger of the two' (p. 135, l. 4) is bitter for her to accept.

Language and Style

Where Ralph is reflective, Undine is business-like in her own way: 'she had done nothing not really necessary' (p. 131, l. 36). There is a new self-awareness in her thoughts now, as when she sees the 'peril' of Van Degen's departure: 'Once off on the *Sorceress*, he was lost to her – the power of old associations would prevail' (p. 133, ll. 15–16). She would not have been capable of this rationalization earlier in the novel, and this calculating element in her character takes her behaviour on to a new level, going beyond the merely instinctive, and working towards 'her advantage' (p. 133, l. 18) more carefully.

Her 'nervous breakdown' (p. 132, l. 7) is in inverted commas. The punctuation allows the reader to question the seriousness of the malaise (perhaps especially if Paul is actually ill). The fact that 'Van Degen's cheque had evidently not brought in the return he expected' (p. 132, ll. 25–6) raises the question what had he expected? Sexual compliance? Ralph has already discounted that possibility. The adverb 'evidently' is interesting, indicating Undine's perception that all is not well.

Note

The Adirondacks (p. 133, l. 31): mountains in upstate New York.

Useful Quotations

'. . . it was admiration she wanted, not love.' (p. 129, l. 4–5)

'At least she had reached the envied situation of the pretty woman with whom society must reckon.' (p. 130, ll. 8–10)

'. . . he would not achieve the quick rise to affluence which was man's natural tribute to woman's merits.' (p. 131, ll. 6–7) (Ralph Marvell)

Chapter XVII, *pp. 135–42*

Focus

This is in effect Undine's rejection of New York, as well as of Ralph. She begins to talk of getting 'free' (p. 139, l. 33), which will continue to be her euphemism for divorce. She uses the social shame that the parents are not invited to dinner as part of her persuasion of her father that she needs to be 'free', but he is not impressed by this argument.

Follow-Up

It is noticeable that Undine goes to her father's office to plead with him this time – an indication of her changing awareness. So her demands and the demands of business are coming closer together. The mention of the 'muddiest reaches of the Pure Water Move' (p. 136, ll. 21–2) neatly brings past and present together, and of course, who should appear but Elmer Moffatt again? It is surely one of Wharton's most obviously ironic moments when he appears just on cue as they are talking of 'the right man' (p. 140, ll. 9–10), although on first reading few readers would pick up the hint, and his mystery is still distant in the past and in the future.

Language and Style

The chapter is full of negative adjectives, most of them 'chosen' by Undine and representing her feelings, from 'bitterer' in the first sentence, through 'galling' (p. 135, l. 16) all the way until the interview when she can take it out on her father. The reader is not sure whether Mr Spragg's comment that 'he'd go and ring the devil's front-door-bell if he thought he could get anything out of him' (p. 142, ll. 3–4) is positive or negative: it might be said with admiration or with disdain. Wharton deliberately leaves that open. He is seen as 'down and out this time' (p. 142, l. 7), and these words are uttered with 'a certain satisfaction'.

There is considerable irony in Mr Spragg's involvement in such 'clean' sounding enterprises as the Pure Water Move and the Fresh Air Fund when, throughout the novel, money is seen as such a corrupting influence.

Useful Quotations

'In the atmosphere of sentimental casuistry to which she had become accustomed, she had forgotten that Mr Spragg's private rule of conduct was as simple as his business morality was complicated.' (p. 137, ll. 28–31)

Chapter XVIII, *pp. 142–56*

Focus

This is the chapter where Undine and Elmer make their deal, Ralph agrees to be involved, despite his vague doubts and reservations, and Undine has her wish to go to Europe. Business and personal motives are now firmly brought together. Undine can afford to behave well now, 'with discretion' (p. 152, l. 24), as she achieves her aims. The result seems positive for Undine, for Ralph and for Elmer – he even talks of 'a fresh start' (p. 154, l. 38).

Follow-Up

There is a certain inevitability in the collusion between Elmer and Undine: it is no coincidence that he has an office in the same building as Mr Spragg. Elmer becomes a figure of fun in society – this is something that will not change, even at the end of the novel. Mrs Fairford's enjoyment of 'provoking him to fresh excesses of slang and hyperbole' (p. 145, ll. 23–4) is a reversal of the impression of him a little earlier as 'a conspicuous and, to some minds, almost a heroic figure' (p. 145, ll. 9–10).

Language and Style

There is more irony in Ralph's reaction to Elmer, 'an amazing fellow' (p. 144, l. 39), 'a kind of epic effrontery' (p. 146, l. 21), especially given the deal they are about to conclude together. The use of the adjective 'Titanic' is curious (p. 146, l. 33): the *Titanic* disaster took place on 14/15 April 1912, which is more or less when Edith Wharton was part way through working on the novel, having restarted work on it in February 1912. She was in Madrid on the night of the disaster. It is not clear whether anything disastrous is implied in the choice of adjective. (In the time-frame of the novel this scene takes place several years before the disaster, so it could be an instance of dramatic irony.)

The final paragraph on p. 150 is a marvellous image from Ralph's past, ironically in Paris, of a lesson in acting, and it reinforces the themes of layers and learning, like 'the secret of an age-long natural process' (p. 150, l. 35). There are very few such references to Ralph's life before Undine (*see* Chapter VI).

The first encounter between Elmer and the young Paul is couched in unusually intimate terms (pp. 153–6). He is surprised that she is planning to go to Europe; he updates her on the burgeoning career of Indiana Frusk, later Mrs Millard Binch, now to be Mrs James J. Rolliver. Money is the key to this divorce and social progress, so it is ironic that it should be Elmer who tells Undine about it (p. 155). Undine's first thought is: 'It showed how easily the thing could be done' (p. 156, ll. 1–2).

Useful Quotations

'The days were not long enough to hold his cares, and they came and stood by him through the silent hours, when there was no other sound to drown their voices.' (p. 148, ll. 9–11) (Ralph Marvell)

'. . . "business" has created its own special morality.' (p. 149, ll. 6–7)

'. . . he was getting to have the drifting dependence on "luck" of the man conscious of his inability to direct his life.' (p. 152, ll. 21–2)

Chapter XIX, *pp. 156–61*

Focus

Charles Bowen resumes his role as commentator, this time from Paris. He finds 'layers upon layers of unsubstantialness' (p. 156, ll. 27–8) in Parisian society. He sees it all as something of a human comedy, a 'phantom' society. Raymond de Chelles is introduced, and ironically comments on the American invention of Parisian society, one of the clearest direct comments on the transatlantic relationship which is a major theme of the novel.

However, the idea of 'institutions' as 'the necessary foundations of society' is also stressed (p. 157, l. 34, l. 35).

Follow-Up

Raymond de Chelles first sees Undine 'at Peter Van Degen's side', (p. 159, ll. 8–9). He thinks she looks unmarried, and this is seen as part of the lack of clarity of each country's custom, which in effect is the subject of the chapter.

Language and Style

Raymond de Chelles is described as coming of 'a family of modest fortune' (p. 158, l. 16), so the reader already knows more than Undine will about that aspect of his life.

The tone of most of the chapter is one of slightly distanced reporting, as is reinforced by the reference to 'the pang of the sociologist' and 'social adjustment' (p. 161, l. 15, l. 16).

In the dialogue it is remarkable that the voices are allowed to speak without constant identification of the speaker. Both speakers are involved in the wittiest line of the chapter: 'marriage', prompts Raymond de Chelles, and Charles Bowen continues that it 'still has its uses. One couldn't be divorced without it' (p. 160, l. 1, l. 3). This is worthy of Oscar Wilde, and is carefully placed almost exactly halfway through the novel when it is still possible to laugh about the divorce customs of Americans.

Useful Quotations

". . . the ideal of the American woman is to be respectable without being bored." (p. 157, ll. 41–p. 158, l. 1)

"Nothing that ever happens here is real." (p. 158, l. 9)

'. . . tonight she seemed to have been brushed by the wing of poetry, and its shadow lingered in her eyes.' (p. 159, ll. 16–18)

(All are Charles Bowen.)

Chapter XX, *pp. 161–72*

Focus

Six weeks have passed, and Undine has a different relationship with Paris compared to the honeymoon. It is 'her first real glimpse into the art of living' (p. 163, l. 41–p. 164, l. 1).

Letters and reporting are important again: her own and Paul's illnesses and the resultant costs bother her. Miss Wincher, last encountered on p. 34, turns up as the Marquise de Trézac. It is pointed out that it is five years since Undine and Peter Van Degen first met, but at the same time as conceding him his first kiss she is now attracted to Chelles. The chapter is largely about these fluctuations of feeling, represented perhaps by 'couples pairing and unpairing again with . . . ease and rapidity' (p. 165, ll. 15–16).

Follow-Up

For the first time Undine is drawn to 'literature', but only because of the potential rewards she has heard about.

The first mention of 'Chelles's chateau in Burgundy' (p. 166, ll. 7–8) ironically comes from Van Degen, emphasizing the web of connections that links the society characters. So, as their closeness grows, the new presence is already noticeable in the background. When the cable about Ralph arrives, Van Degen is aware of her attraction to Chelles. This moment will be returned to much later in the novel. The final lines return to her negative perceptions, even though she has won him. The final sentence is unfinished.

Language and Style

The choice of words is largely Undine's again, especially in terms of her financial concerns and her calling the Marquise de Trézac the 'old enemy' (p. 164, l. 25). Again she is contradictory in her feelings about Van Degen: 'his nearness was not agreeable to Undine, but she liked his free way, his contempt for verbal preliminaries' (p. 167, ll. 23–4), comparing his 'masterful' ways unfavourably with Ralph. (The use of the word 'free', which has such close associations with the subject of divorce, is interesting.)

The kiss is also immediately countered with 'a moment's recoil' (p. 169, l. 1), which is pointedly described as a physical reaction: nothing to do with conscience or scruple.

Useful Quotations

". . . I'm *not* married to you – yet!" (p. 168, l. 2)

"I've got to look out for my future." (p. 171, ll. 39–40)

BOOK THREE

Chapter XXI, *pp. 173–83*

Focus

This is a chapter of displacement and distance: Ralph from Undine, her parents from society and the Stentorian, and even from their grandson, Paul. Even the Lipscombs share the theme, and the reports brought by Mrs Heeny's clippings about New Yorkers in Paris reinforce it.

Reports and letters are how things are communicated in this chapter, so the final communication, the letter from the detective agency, is a serious blow, especially after the ironic tone of much of what has gone before – the novel's irony is becoming more and more serious. The distances are emphasized most significantly in para. 2 on p. 180.

Follow-Up

The passage of time is indicated by Ralph's reflections on 'his present and his former self' (p. 173, ll. 12–13). References to spring traditionally would indicate growth and progress, but this is not what the chapter gives. This is part of the constant contrasts, which are becoming clearer: between aspirations and reality, between capacity and results. In a sense this introduces more strongly the theme of divorce as the way out of an unwanted situation.

Clearly Ralph 'and the boy were no longer part of her life' (p. 175, ll. 31–2). It looks like Undine will go beyond them, but at least that they will be together – this will change later.

Washington Square begins to reassert its presence – it is heavily ironic (but unstated) that as Undine's distance from Ralph grows, the very place that in many ways represents her ambitions is mentioned more. Clare 'who had once been so nearly his' (p. 181, l. 22) begins to assume more importance in Ralph's life. There will from now on be a contrast in how that relationship is handled, compared to Undine's new relationships.

Language and Style

The opening pages are largely reflective, with Ralph's thoughts about himself, his work, his son and his wife. Undine's use of language (p. 174, ll. 1–6) is an unexplained contrast: she does not appear to learn, but does appear to develop her linguistic capacities anyway. And similarly Ralph's language remains static, reflective, rather than proactive, creative, finding new ways, which is Undine's way. Her letters to Ralph express meaningless hope: 'the phrase was always the same' (p. 174, l. 22), indicative of how communication has failed between them. Undine's ways of communicating throughout the novel are encapsulated here: she communicates and performs well when she has a social aim. Where there is nothing to be achieved she does not even bother trying to communicate in more than empty phrases.

Ralph's emotions and physical responses remain, however (p. 174, ll. 32–3). Adjectives like 'penetrating' begin to be used as Ralph's distance from Undine is growing – a contrast therefore between sexual contact as in Chapter XI (the first chapter of Book Two) and sexual distance. The feeling is that the relationship has never been particularly passionate, and Ralph's awareness of this only emerges after the relationship is over, and then only in small touches such as this one.

Again many of Ralph's thoughts end in unfinished sentences. He has doubts about the deal with Elmer Moffatt, and the ambiguity of that arrangement is clear from 'he was not sure there had been anything crooked in that' (p. 176, ll. 10–11) – this doubt is central to the whole novel. The morality of business is always debatable, from Apex to Wall Street, and although the author is never explicit about details of corruption, the kind of older society that Ralph represents will always have these doubts (without reflecting that his own ancestors might have been equally dubious in their financial dealings).

When the subject finally turns to divorce, it is worth noting the adjectives used: 'a vulgar and unnecessary way of taking the public into one's confidence' (p. 182, ll. 34–5). The idea of 'keeping up appearances' is paramount for this kind of society – but not for Undine.

Useful Quotations

'Undine was never at a loss for the spoken word.' (p. 173, l. 35–p. 174, l. 1)

'. . . all she cared for, and attached importance to, was as remote from her parents' conception of life as her impatient greed from their passive stoicism.' (p. 180, ll. 12–15) (Ralph's thoughts on Undine)

Chapter XXII, *pp. 184–90*

Focus

This moves from Ralph's reflections to his disintegration: from thoughts to nightmares, to physical ill-health. Money, and Elmer, emerge as important again. And Undine has finally left Ralph, which is a scandal for Washington Square society.

Follow-Up

The passing of time is mysterious again, indicating something of the lack of clarity in Ralph's perceptions. The distance from New York of the western States is also significant, emphasizing the ideas of displacement from the previous chapter: 'hasn't Dakota been a state for a year or two now?' (p. 188, l. 18). This is a joke at the expense of the newer states, and is anachronistic: North Dakota and South Dakota became states of the Union in 1889.

The reader will probably at this point think, with Ralph, that Undine is to marry Peter Van Degen. This is an important expectation, setting up Undine's reversal in her hopes. Similarly, the reader will probably think that something positive will come of the relationship between Ralph and Clare Van Degen. However, everything about the future is uncertain.

Language and Style

The opening sentence is one of the greatest in the novel: time, emotion and sympathy evoked in fourteen words. It is noticeable how Ralph hears of his wife's leaving him: again it is report, rather than direct information. There is a contrast between the language of the nightmares and the simplicity of the revelation of Undine's departure. Ralph's reaction of anger (p. 189, l. 18ff) probably reinforces the reader's sympathy for him: the outburst is seen as justified, finally a reaction which readers might have wanted him to have much earlier in the story. This is part of the pull of sympathy in the novel – by now Undine has lost sympathy, but perhaps her determination still creates some sense of ambivalent admiration.

It is interesting that another of Undine's victims, her father, has the last word on how to accept and live with the consequences of her action.

Useful Quotations

'When he woke, the first thing he remembered was the fact of having cried.' (p. 184, ll. 34–5)

'Anger was the only emotion in him now.' (p. 189, ll. 18–19)

Chapter XXIII, *pp. 190–95*

Focus

'The moral order of Washington Square' (p. 190, l. 34) and the nature of scandal and report underline Ralph's emotional desolation. There is a clear contrast between the atmosphere of this chapter, opening in the Adirondacks, and the honeymoon chapter in Italy (p. 81ff).

The social reactions and responses to divorce become a focus for satirical comment, between upper-class secrecy and the popular press's trivial discussions.

Follow-Up

The role of Laura (Mrs Fairford, Ralph's sister) begins to take on more importance as she tries to help, and as divorce becomes the dominant theme of the novel.

Language and Style

There is a strong emphasis on silence – scandal is close to non-existence in Washington Square society. The removal of the images of Undine underscores this, although it is done with the best of intentions.

The passage of time is also unspecific – 'Time wore on' (p. 194, l. 18).

The incident of the newspaper on the Subway is perhaps a climax in the ongoing theme of reportage and newspaper stories, bringing together trivia and tragedy (p. 195, l. 1), and how the whole story becomes public property, private emotions being exposed to public gaze and curiosity. The final touch of 'prizes offered' for the solution of the 'Heart problems' (p. 195, ll. 11–13) is one of the strongest satirical comments in the whole novel.

Notes

Lovelace (p. 191, l. 23): in *Clarissa* (1747–1749) by Samuel Richardson, Robert Lovelace is the unscrupulous rake figure with whom the heroine runs off to London, with disastrous consequences.

Sioux Falls (p. 194, l. 22): in South Dakota.

Useful Quotations

'In their vocabulary the word "divorce" was wrapped in such a dark veil of innuendo as no ladylike hand would care to lift.' (p. 191, ll. 9–11)

'. . . a text for pulpit denunciations of the growing craze for wealth.' (p. 195, ll. 8–9)

Chapter XXIV, *pp. 195–204*

Focus

The focus returns to Undine for the first time since the end of Chapter XX. Divorce is the theme, with Indiana Frusk, now Mrs James J. Rolliver, giving Undine advice. This is 'the uttermost depth to which her fortunes had fallen' (p. 195, ll. 25–6).

A year has passed since she was last in Paris, having spent six months in Dakota. And readers' expectations that she might now be married to Peter Van Degen are ended in the conversation about divorce and Van Degen's attitude to it. The reappearance of Miss Wincher of Potash Springs, now the Marquise de Trézac, underlines Undine's failure in her ambitions, and the relationship with Chelles is still uncertain. This is her 'first attempt to reconstruct her past' (p. 201, ll. 40–41), and it is clear that there will be others.

Follow-Up

Undine is convinced that Clare is in love with Ralph. Interestingly the discussion on morality indicates Undine's unwillingness to be 'an immoral woman' (p. 196, l. 38 and p. 200, l. 38) – the repetition makes it clear that her motivation is never purely sexual. The spirits called 'freer' (p. 200, l. 26) might, it is implied, be rather less moral, as was already suggested in the earlier Parisian chapters.

Language and Style

The dialogue is neatly balanced between the strength of Mrs Rolliver's affirmations and the complaints and negativity of Undine's contribution. The fact that the steamer on which Van Degen and the others are reported as having arrived in Europe is the *Semantic* is a witty touch, considering all the semantic discussions going on about the theme of divorce. Indiana seems to take pleasure in announcing that the dinner is 'off' (p. 202, l. 14).

The pronoun 'one' is not much used in the novel, so its use, giving Undine's perception of Indiana Frusk, is worth remarking (p. 199, ll. 22–3). This is part of Undine's understanding of other women. She had considered Indiana Frusk a friend as long as she, Undine, could be superior. Now she is having to adjust her perceptions.

A wider perception is brought into the question of *why* Undine behaved as she did (p. 200, ll. 11–13): 'Since she had not been "sure" of Van Degen, why in the world, they asked, had she thrown away a position she *was* sure of?' The reader might well be minded to ask the same question. This is clever manipulation of point of view – the reader has not been allowed to know Undine's inner feelings and motivations for quite some time, so has to see her through other characters' eyes, and now is the moment of the widest social perspective on her.

Now Undine is 'expected' (p. 201, l. 7) to be various things, and she is perceived as 'the last American divorcée' (p. 200, ll. 30–31). It is important that she is aware of these ways in which she is now being perceived – this is very much a part of the novel where she is coming to terms with how she is seen by others, rather than her own perceptions of herself. She is beginning to learn, about herself and about life. The realization of her misjudgement is perhaps strongest in the very last lines when she hears (again reported, rather than direct) that she was Van Degen's 'ideal'.

Notes

Reno (p. 197, l. 29): in Nevada, still famous for its easy divorces. (*See also* p. 329)

Austrian (p. 199, ll. 13–14): Undine is wrong to call her Austrian. She was introduced as Russian on p. 92.

The reference to Mrs Harvey Shallum (p. 200, l. 13) may not be clear in some editions.

Useful Quotations

'But life had administered some of the discipline which her parents had spared her.' (p. 202, ll. 32–3)

Chapter XXV, *pp. 204–9*

Focus

Perhaps the lowest point in Undine's progress, reinforced by the setting in 'a small quiet place on the Riviera' (p. 205, ll. 23–4). Her memories finally recount the story of her 'two months' with Peter Van Degen (p. 206, l. 35). The brevity of that time contrasts with the opening line of the chapter and its vague sense of time 'over the next few months'. Further references to time (p. 206) reinforce this contrast and the emptiness of her time now.

Follow-Up

Undine wants to get back 'the precise value' of what she has lost (p. 205, l. 6). The contrast with the almost comic tale of 'the gentleman from Little Rock' (p. 208, ll. 36–7 and l. 40) and Mabel's lucky remarriage is striking: it begins to seem that all Undine's oldest friends are doing better than she is.

Language and Style

The paragraphs are longer here, compared to the dialogue of the previous chapter. The feeling is reflective, and comparison might be made with the depiction of Ralph's feelings in Chapters XXI and XXII. She ruminates on her behaviour in terms of 'respectability', 'follies' and 'inexcusable' (p. 206, ll. 35–7), which are new words in her vocabulary.

The use of the word 'honeymoon' (p. 207, l. 41) is a nice ironic contrast with her 'first' honeymoon in Chapter XI.

The Mabel story and Undine's story entwining is wittily underscored by the reference to Undine's reading a novel while 'an actual love-story' is being enacted downstairs (p. 209, ll. 5–7). Her reaction of hate is more like the familiar Undine.

Notes

Tauchnitz (p. 205, l. 35): one of the earliest series of paperback books, in English and other languages, published by Bernhard Tauchnitz, Leipzig.

hid (p. 208, l. 16): in some editions there is a misprint for 'had'.

Useful Quotations

'. . . presently she began to perceive that her companion's view of their relation was not the same as hers.' (p. 207, ll. 14–15)

'He made no sign, he sent no excuse; he simply continued to absent himself.' (p. 209, ll. 3–4)

Chapter XXVI, *pp. 209–17*

Focus

Undine's 'vision' now moves back from where she is, bored, in France, to New York, and it is clear that 'she had learned' a lot in the past few months (p. 209, ll. 28–9), including an appreciation of many positive things about Ralph. Her thoughts move on to custody of the son, Paul. She takes recourse to reading novels – escapism? The escape (p. 210, l. 33) to Europe then becomes reality.

Follow-Up

Mabel's marriage and honeymoon are 'the last touch to Undine's irritation' (p. 211, l. 17) and a return to the opera is commanded, a clear echo of Chapter V. The question of returning the pearls is a significant one: Undine actually listens to her parents on this occasion, but then recovers herself and passes them on to Mrs Heeny to sell them. Again the reader's sympathy is ambivalent. She has an ambition again, to get to Europe, and is motivated by pride to take her parents along with her. But by the end of the chapter she is alone again, in Paris.

Language and Style

Negative words dominate here. At the opera 'nobody noticed her' (p. 211, l. 40), which is quite a contrast with earlier aspirations.

The voices of her parents and Mrs Heeny recall the opening chapters of the novel, this time with the addition, unthinkable then, of her thoughts about her parents accompanying her.

Mr Spragg's judgement of Europe, and of foreigners (i.e. non-Americans) (p. 216, para. 2) are a further contribution to the Europe/America contrast throughout the novel.

The choice of words for the travelling party, 'unnatural association' (p. 216, l. 32) is surprising, and most probably represents Undine's opinion, ironically reported. The reactions of the two Spraggs are nicely contrasted: Mrs Spragg's 'settled terror' (p. 216, l. 34) and Mr Spragg's endless calculations. He now has 'to go back and make the money to pay for all this' (p. 217, ll. 13–14).

Notes

Hecuba (p. 211, l. 33): in the history of Troy, the wife of Priam. In English literature she is portrayed as an extreme example of sorrow.

Useful Quotations

'. . . she gradually began to look on Ralph and herself as the victims of dark machinations, and when she mentioned him she spoke forgivingly.' (p. 210, ll. 26–8)

'. . . foreigners hadn't yet mastered the first principles of time-saving.' (p. 216, ll. 29–30) (Mr Spragg)

Chapter XXVII, *pp. 217–22*

Focus

The story moves back to France and to the present of the story on the Riviera. 'A new life' (p. 219, l. 18) begins to come in with the character of the Princess Estradina, just as Undine considers she is 'at the lowest ebb of her fortunes' (p. 219, l. 25–6).

Follow-Up

Princess Estradina's social connections are made much of – they are not of the highest quality, in terms of the previous chapter's standards

(Madame Adelschein), but the link with Chelles (her cousin) is of major importance. In a variation of the divorce theme 'the Princess was unofficially separated from her husband' (p. 220, l. 24).

Language and Style

Princess Estradina is described in terms like 'boyish' (p. 217, l. 34) and 'the gait of a baker's boy' (p. 219, l. 35). The description of her mother, the Duchesse de Dordogne, as 'like the ruin of a castle' (p. 220, ll. 22–3) is clearly Undine's judgement, and an assertion of her own feeling of some kind of superiority. This all might be a contrast with Undine's flowing wavy femininity, much emphasized early in the novel, but which has been mentioned less and less with the passage of time.

The Princess's English is commented on (p. 217, ll. 34–5), which is unusual in the novel, although the speech patterns of American characters are something Wharton takes great care with. This may underline Undine's position as a step further away from America in the context of the novel as a whole. Estradina also uses more French words in her conversation, which strengthens the Frenchness of the ongoing narration.

Similarly, the reflections on Madame de Trézac reinforce the American/French contrasts. Undine's 'security' (p. 222, l. 1) is immediately undermined: 'her courage fell' (p. 222, l. 7). The final sentence shows she is right to be concerned.

Useful Quotations

'. . . it was instinctive to her to become, for the moment, the person she thought her interlocutors expected her to be.' (p. 219, ll. 4–6)

'Whatever one's errors, one's child belongs to one.' (p. 220, ll. 39–40)

Chapter XXVIII, *pp. 222–26*

Focus

This is the trip to Nice and the glimpse of Elmer Moffatt just before the meeting with Raymond de Chelles. It leads to repeated trips, and

Undine's fortunes can be said to have turned, although, as always, she denies it at first.

Follow-Up

There is clear irony in the contrast between Undine's reaction of 'sincere disgust' (p. 224, l. 13) at what she thinks is 'a clandestine adventure' (p. 224, l. 15) and her own susceptibility to Chelles. Anger and bitterness are still her overriding emotions, especially prompted by seeing Elmer.

Language and Style

The tone of the whole chapter is rather light, brittle, ironic, as if avoiding serious questions. By the end of the chapter, although Undine is refusing to see Chelles, the reader will probably feel the same as the Princess. It is a clever touch on Wharton's part that the reader, for once, feels ahead of Undine in imagining what she wants, and conscious that she is now aware of her own power.

Useful Quotations

'. . . the Princess tried on hats and Undine bought them.' (p. 223, ll. 28–9)

'Undine's increased experience, if it had made her more vigilant, had also given her a clearer measure of her power.' (p. 225, ll. 32–3)

Chapter XXIX, *pp. 227–33*

Focus

Another short chapter, as the story returns to Paris and Undine works on Chelles, but without any calculation in her schemes (presumably her own view of herself). She is happy with the way things are going, and 'ugly memories of failure' (p. 227, l. 31) are being erased. Again time is carefully measured here, as the talk of 'annulment' begins to grow. Family is the main concern, both the family of Raymond de Chelles, including his mother, and Undine's relationship with her own son, who has forgotten what she looks like.

Follow-Up

There is a serious contrast between Undine's implicit aims and the Marquise de Trézac's emphasis on the awareness of traditions in France. Undine is rather dismissive in hoping an American woman ever gets used to French ways (p. 229, l. 3).

The letter from her mother about Paul is another example of distant communication influencing the action of the plot – he does not recognize his mother. The reaction is self-pity, but also determination to have her way.

Language and Style

Although the Marquise de Trézac is American, she appears to have a better perception of France and French ways than Undine will ever have. Undine's reactions are still those of Apex. The importance of keeping up appearances, as in New York society, is an important tenet of how French society works. Undine's failure with Chelles's family is indicative of her outsider status. For her it is 'virtually a declaration of war' (p. 232, l. 41–p. 233, l. 1) and once again she has an aim in view.

Note

There is a slight confusion in Madame de Trézac's information about Raymond's family (p. 232, ll. 8–9). The Duchess is actually Raymond's aunt, not his mother's aunt. The Marquise de Chelles is his mother.

Useful Quotations

'. . . that image of herself in other minds which was her only notion of self-seeing.' (p. 227, ll. 32–3)

"He knows there are traditions he can't fight against – and in his heart he's glad there are." (p. 228, ll. 26–7) (Marquise de Trézac of Raymond de Chelles)

'She was determined to give up Chelles unless he was willing to marry her.' (p. 229, ll. 39–40)

Chapter XXX, *pp. 233–8*

Focus

Another meeting with Elmer Moffatt. The talk is of annulment, and about the child. There is a new emphasis on Elmer's appreciation of Paris, which is very different from Undine's: he will turn into a collector, once he has his millions; the final paragraph of p. 235 is indicative of a sensibility in Elmer which has not emerged until now. He is in Paris 'improving his mind' (p. 237, ll. 30–31), which Undine has not tended to do.

Follow-Up

In what seems an unimportant chapter there are several significant pointers of the future: notably the closeness between Elmer and Undine.

Money will be the key to any annulment of the marriage.

Language and Style

The dialogue between Elmer and Undine is different from those she has with any other character. This is perhaps brought out most clearly with 'Anything I can do for you across the pond?' and her answers (p. 235, ll. 17–23). They have an understanding that allows for an easier level of communication and indeed of subject-matter.

Money and the child remain the final resonances of the chapter.

Useful Quotations

'It never occurred to her that other people's lives went on when they were out of her range of vision.' (p. 234, ll. 4–6)

'He stirred the fibres of a self she had forgotten but not ceased to understand.' (p. 235, ll. 2–3)

BOOK FOUR

Chapter XXXI, *pp. 239–44*

Focus

Although the chapter starts with Ralph and the passing of time (since the divorce), the main event of the chapter is the reported coming marriage of Undine and Raymond de Chelles. Adjustment is the keynote, and again sympathy for Ralph is allowed to develop.

Undine does not actually appear in Book Four, although of course she is ever-present.

Follow-Up

Paul is now six, which is another way of indicating how time has passed.

Ralph's solitude is stressed: 'people left him to his sorrow as a man is left to an incurable habit, an unfortunate tie' (p. 239, ll. 34–5) but it is important to notice that suicide is not a real choice for Ralph.

Clare and Laura are becoming more significant to Ralph now, and literature, objects, anything which can take him out of his thoughts, all begin to assume more importance. The women's concern is where Wharton creates sympathy for Ralph. It is no accident that just after the news of Undine's remarriage Ralph sees the whole thing as 'a part of the huge human buffoonery' (p. 243, l. 30). The fact that the final lines of the chapter bring in the boy, and end in Laura's tears, is a rare moment of sentimentality in the novel. However, it creates a false sense of security about Ralph and Paul staying together and having each other.

Language and Style

It is immensely significant how the unheroic perspective is pointed up: this is very much part of the novel's scope, showing new perspectives on heroes and heroines. How much Undine can be considered a 'heroine' is very much part of what Edith Wharton presumably wants readers to consider – she is a twentieth-century American kind of character, American beauty personified, and her every action questions what the heroine of a novel is or is not. So Ralph's parallel perception of the unheroic nature of his life and his role is crucial, and very much part of the modern tone of the novel (p. 241).

'The smothered springs of life were bubbling up in Ralph' (p. 240, ll. 3–4). The suggestion of creativity and his writing is a kind of displacement activity for any mention of recovering sexual vitality. Like Undine, Ralph is not depicted as a sexual being, although with Clare he is very positive: 'he was more nearly happy with her than with anyone else' (p. 240, ll. 37–38).

The revelation of Undine's remarriage comes just after an 'unusually pleasant' dinner (p. 242, l. 11). The news, and especially the reported and very visual way it is revealed, should come as a shock to the reader, as it does to Ralph, even though it is no real surprise.

Already it is foreshadowed that Undine will be disappointed in Chelles in financial terms, so the reader must be aware that this is not a happy ending or a better career move on her part.

Useful Quotations

'He no longer saw life on the heroic scale; he wanted to do something in which men should look no bigger than the insects they were.' (p. 241, ll. 15–17)

Chapter XXXII, *pp. 244–9*

Focus

Ralph's friendship with Clare is growing, but the question of custody of Paul now looms as a new problem. He will lose him except for access 'at stated intervals' (p. 248, l. 9).

Follow-Up

It is very noticeable that Ralph's hopes are raised only to be dashed again: this allows Wharton to direct the reader's sympathy very strongly to Ralph and Paul. The reader might be as surprised at Ralph that he has thrown away custody of Paul through his own inaction (cf. pp. 193–4).

Language and Style

There is an early emphasis on Ralph's being freer, on the positive aspects of Undine's remarriage. This positive side is, however, immediately undermined by reference to 'his huge immediate wants and feeble vacillating purposes' (p. 244, ll. 25–6). Again, unfinished sentences represent Ralph's indecision and sense of being at a loss as to how to react to the demands from Undine. Once more, the bad news arrives in an indirect way, through a reported telephone call. And again there is a degree of sympathy between Ralph and Mr Spragg.

Useful Quotations

'. . . the spectacle of life seemed less like a dangling of limp dolls.' (p. 245, ll. 10–11)

". . . you're bound to lose in the end." (p. 248, l. 15) (lawyer to Ralph)

Chapter XXXIII, *pp. 249–53*

Focus

Things are moving quite rapidly now. Ralph is beset with contrasting hopes, memories of the past, and the reality of what he cannot do now. Clare's offer to help is a sharp contrast with the kind of 'deal' Elmer could offer.

Follow-Up

Peter Van Degen is in California as all this goes on, so the reader might begin to hope that the relationship between Ralph and Clare could lead to something, especially now that she can help him financially, which is a significant and ironic twist in the male/female relationships in the novel, where it is usually the male who provides the money for the female.

Language and Style

Again the telephone becomes instrumental as it summons Ralph to Mr Spragg's office: letters and the telephone contain the significant messages, face-to-face interviews seem only to confirm the worst.

In the discussion with Clare about Paul, the power of money to 'buy him back from her' (p. 252, l. 14) will by now be seen by the reader, as by Ralph, as a sign of hope, especially since Undine 'wants the money for her annulment' (p. 252, l. 10). The way in which Clare has 'been hoarding up my scrap of income for years' (p. 253, ll. 1–2) is in very sharp contrast with the way Undine spends her money (which is usually provided by other people).

Again the final lines (p. 253), about Clare being able to put 'pressure on' her husband, and the ending of 'bother' are optimistic: the balance between positive and negative is carefully maintained, and the reader must remain as uncertain as Ralph is about the outcome.

Useful Quotations

"I presume you'll have to leave the matter to my daughter." (p. 251, l. 2) (Mr Spragg to Ralph. The earlier reference is to p. 79.)

"She wants him because he'll give her the appearance of respectability." (p. 252, ll. 3–4) (Clare of Undine and Paul)

Chapter XXXIV, *pp. 253–7*

Focus

The power of money is Ralph's main concern, and despite Clare's offer he turns to Elmer. This is where money, risk, and emotional attachment all come together in the novel most directly.

It is the time of 'the reckoning between himself and Undine' (p. 253, ll. 34–5), and it is 'his cousin' who has 'suddenly dominated him' (p. 253, l. 33).

Follow-Up

Wharton cleverly involves the reader in the business element of the story here, because of the presumed sympathy the reader will feel for Ralph's situation. So it is vital that Ralph's attitudes to and perceptions of Elmer and Clare reflect his real concern and anxiety, in contrast with Undine's concerns when she is seeking money, which are wholly selfish. The fact that the various levels of the New York family contribute (Mr Dagonet, his mother and Henley Fairford) is an indication of solidarity which must continue to strengthen the positive hopes Ralph has of keeping Paul.

Language and Style

One of the most remarkable tiny details of physical observation occurs when Ralph notices Elmer's fingers 'with a little black growth on their lower joints' (p. 254, l. 34). There is both fascination and repulsion in this, and irony, given the past connections between Elmer and Ralph, and between Elmer and Undine in the past and the future. The usual physical connotations for Elmer are plumpness and the colour red, so this momentary detail, glimpsed from a masculine perspective, is all the more striking. Elmer is beginning to look and even smell different, and without any pretension, to appreciate good things, such as the little oriental toy (p. 255, l. 6).

It is worth underlining the note of ongoing scandal contained in the 'revival of the Ararat investigation' (p. 254, l. 5), which Ralph is too preoccupied to notice. And Elmer's concern for Paul is also shown (p. 255, l. 37). This will become significant later, and is also a useful counterbalance to Undine's final remark to Elmer on p. 238.

The kiss in the final sentence, and the surroundings of the tapestry and the portrait, bring together some images from the past (society paintings) and the future (the different tapestries at the end of the novel) which give the perhaps unexpected physical act deeper resonances.

Note

'In youth you sheltered me' (p. 255, l. 3): reference to an old popular song 'Woodman, spare that tree,' by G. P. Morris (1802–1864), where the line is 'In youth it sheltered me, And I'll protect it now.' This is a significant indicator of several aspects of Elmer's character: loyalty above all, as well as his cultural terms of reference – a song from more than fifty years before.

Useful Quotations

'That the reckoning between himself and Undine should be settled in dollars and cents seemed last bitterest satire on his dreams: he felt himself miserably diminished by the smallness of what had filled his world.' (p. 253, ll. 34–7)

Chapter XXXV, *pp. 257–65*

Focus

The chapter opens in a state of tense calm: things look like they might be beginning to work out for Ralph, with Clare again 'the comrade of his boyhood' (p. 258, ll. 3–4). He thinks for a few weeks that 'life had freed him from all trammelling delusions' (p. 257, ll. 21). But with Elmer's revelation (p. 263), Ralph's world comes tumbling down.

Follow-Up

What Ralph learns about Elmer is 'more or less contradictory information' (p. 258, l. 16), which is parallel in many ways to how Wharton presents him. But now he has 'come to stay' (p. 258, l. 31), and reached 'permanent eminence' (p. 258, l. 23), both in business and in the novel. Property and culture begin to be mentioned in the context of Elmer, as he begins his rise, and Ralph's downfall is imminent, as the full story of Undine's past relationships comes out.

Language and Style

Calm and silence are the initial modes until the reversal: Ralph is actually waiting for the announcement in the newspapers about the success of his investment. Usually reports have brought bad news: ironic now that silence is just as worrying. It is Henley Fairford who brings word of the project's failure (p. 260, l. 5) – again a report from another person rather than direct information. Then the newspaper report in the *Radiator*, so long awaited, reveals the 'leak'. This is presented simultaneously with another example of Elmer's growing cultural sensibility over 'another little crystal vase' (p. 260, l. 28), like the one on p. 255.

In the discussion of risk, the gap between old society and new is most clearly underscored: for Elmer a few months delay is nothing, for Ralph it is a huge problem. This particular dialogue is one of the most carefully handled in the entire novel, reaching a tremendous climax, which should be a surprise to the reader (despite a certain inevitability to it) as it is to Ralph: 'the fact that I've been divorced from Mrs Marvell' is trumped with Elmer's 'I've been divorced from her myself' (p. 263, ll. 13–14 and ll. 18–19). It is also supremely ironic that the cause of the heated exchange is Elmer Moffatt's remark about Undine and money – his understanding of her, and Ralph's understanding of her are quite different, and it is clearly Elmer who knows her better.

The full story can now be told, and is told in a very summary and matter-of-fact way: no melodrama, no scandal, just the facts of her marriage to Elmer and her engagement to Millard Binch, 'the same she passed on to Indiana Rolliver' (p. 264, ll. 4–5). The marriage to Elmer in Opake, Nebraska was 'nine years ago last month' (p. 264, ll. 1–2), one of the most specific time references in the novel, and was 'a year or two' after that early engagement. Opake nicely conveys also the hidden nature of this relationship, which has coloured the whole novel, and makes both Ralph and the reader go back to reconsider Elmer's role throughout.

Powerful influences caused them to unloop 'the loop' (p. 264, l. 14), and the story of marriage and divorce is contained within one paragraph – almost a microcosm of the entire novel. It is interesting that Elmer thereafter went to Alaska, as far away as possible but still in the United States, while the next year the Spraggs moved to New York. The irony that Elmer then next met Undine at the theatre on the day 'your engagement was announced' (p. 264, ll. 17–18) is almost the supreme closing of the ironic circle.

Ralph's reaction is perhaps unexpected, returning to Elmer's 'vulgarity' (p. 264, l. 22) and his physical presence, and blowing him up to monstrous proportions. Elmer even seems not to recall the first time they met (which may well be discretion on his part). The final paragraphs, with Ralph's recurring unfinished phrases, emphasize the totality of the crash that has hit him. It is *not* portrayed as Elmer's triumph, however: Ralph allows defeat to overwhelm him.

Notes

'Voice that Breathed o'er Eden' (p. 264, l. 7): from a poem entitled 'Holy Matrimony' by John Keble (1792–1866). It is a sign of how carefully Wharton makes such references that the lines read, 'The voice that breathed o'er Eden,/ That earliest wedding day.'

Alaska (p. 264, l. 15): Alaska was bought by America from Russia in 1867; it became a full state of the Union only in 1959, so is appropriately far from the current United States at the time the novel is set.

Useful Quotations

"I've been divorced from her myself." (p. 263, ll. 18–19)

'. . . the irrelevance of all the old attitudes of appropriation and defiance . . . stumbling about in his inherited prejudices like a modern man in medieval armour . . . the whole archaic structure of his rites and sanctions came tumbling down about him.' (p. 265, ll. 7–13)

Chapter XXXVI, *pp. 265–8*

Focus

A brief coda to the previous chapter, tracing Ralph's confused thoughts and memories (the honeymoon scenes again): shock and incomprehension are his reactions.

Follow-Up

Ralph is the character whose thoughts the reader has been allowed to share, so the final image should come as something of a shock, despite whatever sympathy the reader feels for him.

Language and Style

Ralph still feels some positive attraction for Undine (p. 266, ll. 34–8), even at the moment of his greatest despair.

The contrast between the now familiar tracing of Ralph's thoughts in free indirect speech and report of thoughts is very neatly interrupted by the distraction of the parlour-maid and her inconsequential chat. The portentous final thought that 'this will make it all right for her' (p. 268, ll. 22–3) might be seen as a little melodramatic, but is Ralph's final gesture towards Undine, and he wants to see it as positive.

Useful Quotation
'She had lied to him – lied to him from the first.' (p. 266, l. 32)

BOOK FIVE

Chapter XXXVII, *pp. 269–75*

Focus
Without referring directly to the previous chapter, the action has moved to France and opens with another of Wharton's descriptions of an interior. Only the reference to the 'little boy in mourning' (p. 269, l. 4) gives the reader the clue.

The action will now largely be in France, and Undine is already married to Raymond de Chelles.

There will be a recurring theme of contrasts between America and Paris, but economy and lack of money remain a preoccupation. By the end of the chapter her rather ambiguous contentment is threatened, as Raymond is insisting on leaving Paris.

Follow-Up
As with Undine's marriage to Ralph, this transition should represent an achievement, a possibility of settled happiness, but already there are negative aspects to it. It is gradually revealed that the now married Chelles are staying with Raymond's father, so accommodation is again a problem, as it has been from the very beginning of the novel.

The 'definite and complicated code of family prejudices and traditions' (p. 271, ll. 30–31) is not far from the Washington Square code of conduct in the early chapters.

Language and Style
Time is revealed only gradually: Undine and Raymond have been married for three months; Undine and Paul have been separated for three years; Undine had been alone for two years; and after Ralph's death 'had released her' (p. 274, l. 24) there was 'the lapse of a year' (p. 274, ll. 34–35) before her marriage. These time shifts, moving back and forward between present and past, leave the reader with a deliber-

ately vague idea of how much time has passed, and the relative importance of the things that have happened, especially to Undine herself. It is particularly ironic that the money Ralph was waiting for did come through, 'about three months after Ralph's death' (p. 274, ll. 38–39) – considerable wealth, provided, of course, through Elmer. Time and money reach a peak of interconnection here.

Undine is now 'in the flush of a completer well-being than she had ever known' (p. 270, ll. 32–33). She describes her husband as 'charming'; he reminds her of Ralph, which merits an exclamation mark, representing her own surprise at the fact. And above all she is 'adored and protected' (p. 270, l. 41).

All of this gives the reader the impression of a comfortable marriage rather than a love relationship, and indeed some discrepancy of outlook is revealed when the word 'love' is used, of Raymond (p. 271, l. 13). Her memories seem to deny what Chapter XXXV had revealed about her marriage to Elmer – clearly she has eliminated that from 'her sentimental memories' (p. 271, ll. 10–11).

It is only towards the middle of the chapter that linguistic terms are brought into consideration: 'she was no longer a divorced woman . . . but a widow' (p. 272, ll. 14–16), and suddenly Ralph's death is made actual in the changed perspectives it has created for Undine and for those in France who judge her. Ralph's death itself is referred to, again outside the logical sequence of time, in appropriately unfinished sentences and phrases, and the word suicide is carefully avoided (p. 274, ll. 24–31). The Chelles family suddenly have no more objections to the marriage, 'discovering' her 'merits' (p. 272, ll. 29–30), despite Madame de Trézac's rather double-edged affirmation that she is 'what *we* call rich in America' (p. 272, ll. 38–9). The reader might treat all this with some scepticism, especially when it is said later that she 'somewhat conspicuously adopted her husband's creed' (p. 275, ll. 8–9) – the adverbial phrase making the narrator's stance clear.

Madame de Trézac's 'militant patriotism' (p. 272, l. 41) sets the tone here: the Americans are as much a target of irony as the French are. Neither side is portrayed in a particularly positive light. This is most definitely not a novel of European superiority to America, as many of Henry James's novels, and indeed some of Edith Wharton's later novels are. It is more a novel of an individual in both societies than a novel comparing and contrasting the two societies to the detriment of one.

Madame de Trézac's idea that 'a woman must adopt her husband's nationality whether she wants to or not' (p. 273, ll. 22–3) raises a problem. Mrs Heeny's 'democratic ease' (p. 273, l. 40) is one of the few pointed contrasts between new America and old France: she has had this ease throughout the novel, and one of her characteristics is her ability to move in various levels of society because of her profession: 'in that character she felt herself entitled to admission to the highest circles' (p. 274, l. 2–3).

The final paragraph (p. 275) is a fine example of Wharton's ability to bring together positives and negatives, and move the story forward into an unpromising future.

Note

Shatter-country (p. 274, l. 12): Mrs Heeny's idiosyncratic pronunciation of chateau-country.

Useful Quotations

'. . . she continued to wish that she could have got what she wanted without having had to pay that particular price for it.' (p. 274, ll. 35–6)

'. . . one more instance of the perverseness with which things she was entitled to always came to her as if they had been stolen.' (p. 275, ll. 23–5)

Chapter XXXVIII, *pp. 276–84*

Focus

Saint Désert (which is about 10 km west of Chalon-sur-Saône) becomes a symbolic desert for Undine. The echoes of Dickens's *Bleak House* are almost palpable, as the old Marquis dies and French ways, traditions and codes take over her life as her 'long months' there become 'a monotonous blur' (p. 276, ll. 21–2).

Follow-Up

The chapter slowly builds up to Raymond's resistance to Undine (p. 279) and to the 'new cataclysm' (p. 279, l. 41) of her brother-in-law Hubert's marriage to an American and the passing of her hoped-for home in Paris to them. Her rejection of Raymond and Saint Désert at the end of the chapter is total, and also implies the end of their sexual relationship.

Language and Style

The early part of the chapter is in long slow paragraphs, reinforcing the sense of static boredom felt by Undine. Her disappointment at the division of her father-in-law the old Marquis's property is the crux of the problem with the Paris house. Hubert's 'scandalous prodigalities' (p. 280, l. 10) are an echo of Undine's spending – but he is rescued by an American connection. And it is heavily ironic that the new tenants will bring twentieth-century improvements to the place: 'the understanding that he puts electric light and heating into the whole *hôtel*' (p. 283, ll. 3–4). It is ironic too, that Hubert's American wife, Miss Looty Arlington, has a name which is even more absurd than Undine's – 'What a name!' she herself says (p. 281, l. 21), although it is almost the same as what her father calls her mother (*see* p. 74). And Miss Looty Arlington comes from 'some new state . . . not yet . . . on the map . . . already known as one of 'the divorce states''' (p. 282, ll. 5–7). (*See* Note below.)

The move into dialogue reinforces the crisis, and it is no coincidence that there is mention of 'your customs' (p. 282, l. 13), although it is perhaps surprising that the mention should come from Undine herself.

The tapestries in the 'long grey gallery' (p. 281, l. 3; *see also* p. 291, l. 27) will assume great significance during the rest of the novel.

Notes

Utah became a state in 1896, Oklahoma in 1907, Arizona and New Mexico in 1912. The likely time-frame of the novel suggests that Looty Arlington comes from one of the last two new states.

Boucher (p. 280, l. 38): François Boucher (1703–1770), Parisian painter and engraver, designed *cartons* to be made into tapestries at the Parisian factories of Beauvais and Gobelins. He was a court painter to Louis XV (*see* p. 166, ll. 13–14).

General Arlington (p. 281, l. 27): there is a note of snobbery here. Looty Arlington's father seems to have no military connections; he is only a General Manager (p. 281, l. 28), therefore one of the new rich.

Useful Quotations

'A harmless instance of transatlantic oddness.' (p. 277, ll. 37–8)

'She was beginning to see that he felt her constitutional inability to understand anything about money as the deepest difference between them.' (p. 279, ll. 2–4)

Chapter XXXIX, *pp. 284–91*

Focus

The threat at the end of the previous chapter is immediately contradicted: a year has passed, the house in Paris has been modernized and transformed, and Undine has developed a new 'stoicism' in the face of 'circumstances stronger than any effort she could oppose to them' (pp. 284, l. 27, ll. 28–9). Her power over Raymond has subtly changed now; she has 'a startled sense of not giving him all he expected of her' (p. 285, ll. 13–14). Raymond begins to be active in politics and Undine is often left in Saint Désert.

This leads to a distance between them, and Undine's innocence at the implications is commented on by Princess Estradina, talking of Americans in general: 'you're the only innocent women left in the world . . .' (p. 291, ll. 12–13).

Follow-Up

Family and 'the conditions of her new life' (p. 288, l. 22) begin to concern Undine more than ever before. Time-shifts between past and present echo the moves between Saint Désert and Paris.

Language and Style

This is largely recounted in long paragraphs, with only brief moments of dialogue – it is a process of reassessment and recognition.

The avoidance of the subject of childlessness underlines the distance between Undine and Raymond, and her 'wounded pride' (p. 287, l. 31) at Raymond's turning away from her is a direct echo of the scene between Ralph and Undine at the end of Chapter XV (p. 127).

The story of their travels, and the family's comments on it, show how Undine does not fit in, but finally she comes 'to understand the fundamental necessity of these things being as they were' (p. 290, ll. 6–7).

Useful Quotations

'. . . she . . . was mortified by the discovery that there were regions of his life she could not enter.' (p. 285, ll. 35–7)

'It was natural that the Americans, who had no homes, who were born and died in hotels, should have contracted nomadic habits.' (p. 289, ll. 5–7)

'. . . a powerful and indivisible whole, the huge voracious fetish they called The Family.' (p. 289, ll. 29–31)

Chapter XL, *pp. 291–7*

Focus

Stultification at Saint Désert continues for Undine, and Raymond's indifference grows. She lapses 'into an apathy' (p. 294, l. 22) like her mother's, affirming Oscar Wilde's dictum in *The Importance of Being Earnest*, 'All women become like their mothers. That is their tragedy. No man does. That is his.'

Follow-Up

The question of the firewood becomes an emblem of the relationship between Undine and her mother-in-law.

Language and Style

The language chosen to describe 'one of the chief distractions of her new life would be to invent ways of annoying her mother-in-law' (p. 292, ll. 5–7) indicates little sympathy for Undine's plight. 'The blank surface of his indifference' (p. 293, l. 17) is contrasted with words like 'amiable' and the narrator accentuates the ongoing good manners and keeping up appearances.

Again dialogue leads to the climax, with money at the heart of the problem: the monetary value of the tapestries is mentioned by Undine, and that leads to Raymond's final words.

Useful Quotations

'The dullness of her life seemed to have passed into her blood.' (p. 294, l. 10)

'. . . she could not conceive that any one could tire of her of whom she had not first tired.' (p. 295, ll. 21–3)

'. . . the clue to their whole unhappy difference.' (p. 297, l. 4)

Chapter XLI, *pp. 297–303*

Focus

This is where Undine tries to sell the tapestries. The appearance of the dealer, Mr Fleischhauer, with his 'swarthy . . . odd exotic air' (p. 298, ll. 25–6) is a rather racist touch to today's ear. The surprise is the appearance of Elmer: 'this gentleman buys only things that are not for sale' (p. 299, ll. 17–18). Elmer's appearance, when the dealer calls him, is a nicely handled theatrical moment.

Follow-Up

This is the turning-point chapter, and from now on the movement towards the denouement is fairly rapid. Elmer reappears as something of a conquering hero, his conquest being represented by his financial triumphs, which are recounted on pp. 301–3. He wants the tapestries for his private railway car – this is emblematic of the kind of wealth Elmer represents: he has made his fortune in the modern communications industry of the time, railways. The pronoun 'one' is used to delineate something of Undine's reaction to Elmer's new-found wealth (p. 301, l. 9). Her judgement is that 'It must have come about very recently, yet he was already at ease in his new honours' (p. 301, ll. 12–13).

Language and Style

The conversation between Undine and Elmer establishes 'some underlying community of instinct' (p. 302, ll. 9–10). Tribalism and materialism begin to coincide, and it is no accident that Wharton underlines the language aspect of their closeness: 'Here was someone who spoke her language, who knew her meanings, who understood instinctively all the deep-seated wants for which her acquired vocabulary had no terms' (p. 302, ll. 21–3).

She finally confesses her loneliness, he tells his story, and his passion for collection emerges: they share the desire for 'the best' (p. 303, l. 28).

Note

Desdemona ... anthropophagi (p. 303, ll. 3–4): in Shakespeare's *Othello*, Desdemona marries Othello because she has been impressed by his stories of victories against the Cannibal and 'the Anthropophagi, and men whose heads/ Do grow beneath their shoulders'.

Useful Quotations

'To have things had always seemed to her the first essential of existence.' (p. 303, ll. 10–11)

Chapter XLII, *pp. 303–8*

Focus

Back in Paris, this chapter is the heart of France/America contrasts, with 'relations' a key to 'the whole of French social life' (p. 304, l. 15).

Follow-Up

In plot terms, it is the proposed sale of the tapestries that brings the cultural and personal contrasts to a head. Raymond 'had known' (p. 306, l. 33) about the visit to Saint Désert, and Undine tries to justify herself with excuses of economy. This brings Raymond to the crisis line: '. . . that's all you feel when you lay hands on things that are sacred to us!' (p. 307, ll. 11–12).

Language and Style

Again there is a particular stress laid on language in Raymond's reactions: 'You come among us speaking our language and not knowing what we mean' (p. 307, ll. 18–19). This whole paragraph is crucial to the contrasts between the two countries: the newness ('where the streets haven't had time to be named'). Raymond's refusal to sell (echoes of 'I repudiate it, *thus*') is the moment he loses Undine.

Useful Quotations

'But it was impossible for Undine to understand a social organization which did not regard the indulging of women as its first purpose.' (p. 306, ll. 8–10)

'. . . the people are as proud of changing as we are of holding to what we have.' (p. 307, ll. 24–25) (Raymond de Chelles on America, compared to France)

Chapter XLIII, *pp. 308–13*

Focus

This is the return in memory and then in reality to Undine's first marriage partner. It is also the chapter which is most clearly ironic about America and its history, or lack of history.

Follow-Up

Even the graveyards of Saint Désert seem to be conspiring against Undine (p. 308, ll. 27–30), so a return to her 'brief adventure' (p. 309, l. 8) with Elmer Moffatt is both a return to the past and an enticing temptation for the future.

Language and Style

Just as the circle is coming to completion, one essential mystery is left wide open: 'No one in Apex knew where young Moffatt had come from, and he offered no information on the subject' (p. 309, ll. 21–2). This is part of what makes America a country without a past, and this remains one of the major differences between America and France, where there is considerable insistence on the past – witness the gravestones at Saint Désert.

The story of the Apex romance is actually the closest resemblance to a traditional novel, and deliberately contains references to early American history, the distant American past of George Washington (only some 160 years before the action of the novel). That these are handled in a comic context is an indication of Wharton's irony about her native land. The fact that the park where the lovers walked is 'immature' (p. 312, l. 26) is another sign of America's lack of history and development, which is reinforced by the mention of its temporary, moveable architecture in Apex (p. 308, ll. 18–19). It is of course ironic that the celebration where it all happens is the Fourth of July, and even more so that Elmer gets drunk at a Temperance Society event.

Elmer emerges as an attractive and spirited character in this chapter, in marked contrast with practically every other character in the novel.

Notes

the Blue and the Grey (p. 310, l. 9): historical reference: the northern Unionist army in the American Civil War (1861–1865) wore blue, the southern Confederates grey.

Washington and the Cherry Tree (p. 310, l. 10): the legend that America's first President, George Washington could not tell a lie about cutting down a cherry tree.

Bartlett (p. 310, l. 14): the standard American Dictionary of Quotations.

smilax (p. 310, l. 24) : a decorative kind of asparagus fern plant.

the Limited (p. 313, l. 19): a train, heading west (i.e. into the new and unknown).

Useful Quotations

'Undine . . . tasted the public triumph which was necessary to her personal enjoyment.' (p. 309, ll. 37–9)

'Success was beauty and romance to her.' (p. 312, ll. 15–16)

Chapter XLIV, *pp. 313–19*

Focus

The return to the present in Paris is signalled by the reference to Undine's 'husband' (p. 313, l. 26) – the reader might be forgiven for wondering *which* husband she is referring to, but of course it is the current one, Raymond. The confusion will be further justified as money problems and tensions with Raymond and his family bring her closer and closer to Elmer.

Follow-Up

Undine is not trying so hard now 'to see her compatriots' (p. 314, l. 14), a sign that she is becoming a little less dependent on social relations with others. The tension between herself and Raymond's family might be seen as echoing tensions between America and France, but Wharton does not stress this too much.

Language and Style

Again Undine's and Elmer's tastes are seen as coinciding, although Elmer's cultivated taste and his interest in art and collecting underline their cultural differences. His 'aesthetic emotions' and 'the great steel strong-box of his mind' (p. 318, l. 1; ll. 2–3) are impenetrable to Undine. How they 'use' life is similar, however, and that is the main thing that draws them together.

The contrast with Raymond is clear: he is concerned with keeping up appearances (p. 318, ll. 7–9, *see* below), although this is not criticized as hypocritical – it is simply how his class behaves, and would not be very different from Washington Square Society's codes. His family is united in concealing the 'blot on their honour' (p. 319, l. 1).

It is significant that Undine does not want to 'use' Elmer: she sees him as 'one who knew her and understood her grievance' (p. 319, ll. 14–15). As she goes to him at the end of the chapter, the decision seems inevitable, and she has now decided 'to keep him for herself alone' (p. 319, ll. 28–9).

Note

Ingres (p. 316, l. 2): French Classicist painter (1780–1867). (Elmer's tastes tend more towards the Classical than the Romantic.) Elmer buys the painting from Raymond de Chelles's uncle, who is Princess Estradina's father.

Useful Quotations

"Oh, he despises Americans – they all do." (p. 315, l. 34) (Undine to Elmer, about Raymond and the French in general)

'He used life exactly as she would have used it in his place.' (p. 317, ll. 31–2) (Elmer Moffatt)

'. . . it was an article of his complicated social creed that a man of his class should appear to live on good terms with his wife.' (p. 318, ll. 7–9) (Raymond de Chelles)

Chapter XLV, *pp. 319–24*

Focus

The chapter of decisions: Undine's sincerity is stressed, her 'self-interest was in abeyance' (p. 320, l. 27), and the closeness of her feelings to how she felt years ago with Elmer is repeated.

Follow-Up

Undine is less decisive, selfish and demanding in her conversations here – her emotions are finally seen as possibly genuine where Elmer is concerned. In effect, the decision is Undine's but Elmer pushes it just a little towards the end of the chapter.

Language and Style

The chapter opens with another Wharton interior, this time described in terms of the things Elmer has collected, all of which are identified by their historical connections: from Renaissance to Phoenician to Greek. Elmer has no history, so he buys it – but appreciates it too.

The reader must decide how much to believe Undine when she claims that 'It's the only time I ever really cared – all through!' (p. 321, ll. 13–14) and 'I've always felt, all through everything, that I belonged to you' (p. 321, l. 32).

Elmer is quite matter-of-fact in his responses, but interestingly it is her American-ness to which his final appeal is made, and in an American idiom: 'ain't you?' (p. 324, l. 17). He wins the test of nerves, and the voyage back, again on the *Semantic*, can be expected to include Undine, on her way to another divorce.

Useful Quotations

'. . . she felt again, as she had felt that day, the instinctive yearning of her nature to be one with his.' (p. 320, ll. 27–28)

"They think so differently about marriage over here: it's just a business contract." (p. 321, ll. 29–30)

'It seemed to her that the great moment in her life had come at last.' (p. 322, ll. 40–41)

"Who cares what they do over here? You're an American, ain't you? What you want is the home-made article." (p. 324, ll. 16–17) (Elmer to Undine)

Chapter XLVI, *pp. 325–35*

Focus

The final chapter, but with no sense of closure or finality. Again it opens with an interior, but seen this time through the eyes of Paul Marvell, now nearly nine years old. He becomes a major character in this chapter: his loneliness and his very ambivalent prospects as 'the richest boy in America' (p. 332, l. 30) underscore Undine's lack of concern for her son, and question the value of her success. Despite her own sense of achievement, she leaves victims everywhere.

Follow-Up

The full extent of how carefully plotted the whole novel is only becomes clear now: the significance of Paul for the future and Elmer for the past, the presence of Mrs Heeny at the beginning and end of the story, the purchase of the tapestries and the decline in Raymond's fortunes (through an American bankruptcy, rather than any French influence), the appointment of 'that pitiful nonentity' Jim Driscoll (p. 334, l. 28) as ambassador to London, all of these lead to the remarkably open conclusion, which in turn could easily be the opening of another novel.

Language and Style

The emptiness of Paul's life makes a strong impact here, and this reinforces the distance with which Undine is viewed. The divorce and remarriage are again revealed only through Mrs Heeny's cuttings and newspaper reports: indirect rather than direct narration has been the mode throughout. The energy of the railroad and train references in the report of the divorce is striking (p. 330, ll. 6–18), especially since Elmer is now described as 'the billionaire Railroad King'. The first marriage is now also public news, although not actually commented on (p. 330, ll. 4–5). The date of this report, 23 November, is unusual in being so precise (p. 329, l. 41) – in practical terms it brings the story right up to date.

The fact that the information about Jim Driscoll comes from a discarded newspaper is also neat, and allows Wharton to give Undine's choice of adjectives predominance in the final pages. Her narcissism is again stressed as 'according to her invariable habit' (p. 334, l. 8) she studies her image in the mirror.

When she compares her current husband with her previous two, 'the comparison was almost always to Moffatt's disadvantage' (p. 333, ll. 38–9). This is not the happy marriage conclusion to a novel – Elmer is only given his surname now. Wharton leaves the reader with the taste of Undine's lack of contentment and lack of satisfaction. The lies she has told about Raymond, in the press and to her son, remain also as evidence against her in her moment of triumph. The reader is almost challenged, right to the end, in terms of how much sympathy can be felt for this anti-heroine.

The final image, of a new beginning, is heavily underscored by the disappointment at what she cannot be and cannot have, all of which is due to the fact that she ever divorced Elmer in the first place. The circle is complete, but Undine's ambitions remain unfulfilled.

Notes

Vandyck (p. 329, l. 7): British court painter (1599–1641).
Velasquez (p. 334, l. 15): Spanish painter (1599-1660).

Useful Quotation

'Under all the dazzle a tiny black cloud remained.' (p. 335, l. 13)

Characters

Relationships and Names

Undine Spragg is the central figure around whom everything revolves. Her name suggests a figure from European mythology, an elemental spirit, a water-sprite, a creature without a soul, who can only acquire a soul by marrying a mortal and bearing him a child. Her treatment of her son, Paul, would seem to confirm that not even by marrying does this Undine acquire a soul. The name is used by Friedrich de la Motte Fouqué in a Romantic tale of 1811 which was the basis for several successful operas including, in 1816, one by E. T. A. Hoffmann (1776–1822), and another in 1845 by Albert Lortzing (1801–1851).

Her surname has some levels of meaning potential as well: 'sprag' is defined, among other things as 'a twig', 'a stout piece of wood inserted between the spokes of a wheel as a stop', 'a lively young fellow', 'a young fish'. As an adjective it carries connotations of 'smart' or 'clever'.

In the novel her mother tells her future husband that she is named after 'a hair-waver father put on the market the week she was born' (p. 48), so her name is associated with the market-place from her very birth.

Undine's parents

Abner E. Spragg and *Leota B. Spragg* (called Loot by Abner). They come with her to New York to get away from the past in Apex.

Undine's husbands

Elmer Moffatt, who came from nowhere (p. 309). He is red and plump and a risk-taker.

Ralph Marvell, grandson of Urban Dagonet, is a dilettante who has never worked.

Raymond de Chelles, who becomes Marquis de Chelles; he is later involved in politics.

Their families

Ralph's mother, *Mrs Paul Marvell*, daughter of Urban Dagonet.

Ralph's sister, *Laura*, Mrs Henley Fairford.

Ralph's cousin *Clare*, née Dagonet, wife of Peter Van Degen, who is also close to Ralph.

Ralph and Undine's son *Paul Marvell,* who is conceived in Paris.

Raymond's parents, *the Marquis and Marquise* (later Dowager Marquise).

Raymond's brother, *Hubert*, who marries *Looty Arlington.*

Raymond's cousin, *Princess Lily Estradina*, daughter of the Duchesse de Dordogne, becomes Undine's friend.

Undine's Friends, Lovers and Servants

Undine's lover *Peter Van Degen*, is the son of a banker, Thurber Van Degen, and the husband of Clare.

Undine's Apex fiancé, *Millard Binch*, is a druggist's clerk. Later he marries *Indiana Frusk*, a plumber's daughter, who divorces him to marry Representative *James J. Rolliver.*

Undine's boarding-school friend from New York, *Mabel Lipscomb*, née Blitch, who gives Undine her first introduction to New York society. She later divorces Harry Lipscomb and marries 'the man from Little Rock', Homer Branney.

Undine's masseuse and manicurist *Mrs Heeny*, who later brings Paul to Europe and is with him at the end of the story. The source of much information and gossip from the newspapers.

Undine's French maid, *Céleste*, is her earliest contact with France.

Undine's holiday acquaintance in Potash Springs, *Nettie Wincher* from Washington D.C., later the *Marquise de Trézac* or *Madame de Trézac*, is already divorced from her French husband when Undine meets her again in Paris.

New York characters

Charles Bowen, a 'hopelessly elderly' (p. 22) ascetic New York and Paris socialite, close to Laura and Clare. The first character to meet Raymond de Chelles, he introduces Raymond to Undine.

Harmon B. Driscoll employs Elmer Moffatt as his private secretary. Elmer calls him 'Uncle Harmon B' (p. 66).

Jim Driscoll 'heir apparent of the house' (p. 112); husband of *Mamie*. Becomes US Ambassador to England (p. 334).

Claude Walsingham Popple, New York society painter.

Harriet Ray, a desiccated unmarried socialite (p. 176, l. 30).

European characters

Sacha Adelschein, a Russian aristocrat, friend of Princess Estradina.

Count or *Marchese Roviano*, an Italian nobleman Undine meets on her honeymoon.

The *Shallums*, Bertha and Harvey, Americans resident in Paris.

Mr Fleischhauer, dealer in works of art.

Critical Viewpoints on the Novel

This novel seems to attract praise and negative comments in almost equal measure. Edith Wharton's most recent biographer, Shari Benstock, says that it was *The Custom of the Country* which cost Edith Wharton the Nobel Prize for Literature in the 1920s, when she was at the peak of her fame and success. Benstock quotes Kenneth Clark as saying that the Swedish prize committee found the novel 'too cynical'. This has often been the main thrust of comments on the novel: Harold Bloom calls it 'Wharton's strongest achievement', but goes on to say that it is 'rather an unpleasant novel to reread'.

Most of the criticism of the novel sways between this kind of admiration tempered with reservations about the tone of the book and the lack of sympathy readers feel for Undine Spragg.

Influences and Contexts

It is important to see how Edith Wharton saw this novel in relation to the traditions of the theme of marriage and achievement. Marriage has been a major theme in fiction from the very beginning of the novel's popularity as a genre in the early eighteenth century. Frequently this is said to have been because of the fact that the majority of readers of novels were women. The traditional way of approaching marriage in the novel, epitomized by Samuel Richardson, whose *Clarissa* is referred to in Chapter XXIII, is that its consummation is to be devoutly wished, as it is the objective of any unmarried female, especially if it is to a man with money. Of course, *Clarissa*, like so many other novels of the time, was written by a man. Dale Spender in *Mothers of the Novel: 100 good woman writers before Jane Austen*, usefully reminds us that there were many women also writing at the time, although their works did not necessarily reach the wide readership of Richardson, Defoe and Fielding.

In many ways the novels of Jane Austen are the epitome of this kind of 'happy ending' approach, although of course in her case it is always tempered with her own particular brand of irony. In the Victorian period there is a shift of emphasis as women become more aware of their roles. The climax of Charlotte Brontë's *Jane Eyre,* 'Reader, I married him', moves the focus on to the woman's capacity to make major decisions: the female narrator is the subject, the husband the object. Jane refuses the option of becoming Rochester's mistress (as Undine does with Peter Van Degen). She is not just a sexual object, as she might have been a century earlier in *Clarissa*, or a sexual and social victim, like Daniel Defoe's Moll Flanders or Roxana.

Edith Wharton was very well read, and the influences of her reading appear in many ways in *The Custom of the Country*. Wharton admired George Eliot and especially *Middlemarch* a great deal. One of her publishers, Charles Scribner, thought Wharton would be 'the George Eliot of her time'. The critic Q. D. Leavis compared the two: 'Undeniably Mrs Wharton had a more flexible mind, she was both socially and morally more experienced than George Eliot and therefore better able to enter into uncongenial states of feeling and to depict as an artist instead of a preacher distasteful kinds of behaviour. Her Undine Spragg is better sustained and handled than the other's Rosamund Vincy.' For Leavis, perhaps as expected, George Eliot emerges as the greater writer. There are rarely remarked but distinct echoes of Eliot's *Middlemarch* on pp. 88 and 127 of *The Custom of the Country*, emphasizing the loneliness of the newly married heroine. Balzac was another writer Wharton admired immensely, and it is easy to detect both explicit and implicit traces of *la comédie humaine* throughout the novel, as well as particular hints of some of Balzac's writing where money and social ambition coincide – *Eugénie Grandet* is perhaps the most obvious of these influences.

It is interesting that Edith Wharton also admired and indeed loved George Sand, but did not own any of her novels. She was fascinated by strong female personalities and their successes, but did not necessarily take to the creative results of their work. However, she and Henry James shared a great devotion to Sand and visited her shrine at Nohant together more than once.

Wharton's name and reputation have always been closely associated with Henry James. They were good friends, and travelled a lot together in the first decade of the century. But it is mistaken to see them as very similar in their styles of writing, or in their ways of handling their subject matter. Edith Wharton did not like James's later novels, finding the writing too elaborate for her tastes – she always has the virtue of simplicity and conciseness, something she had admired in Henry James's earlier novels, such as *Washington Square*. It is a novel which inevitably resonates through *The Custom of the Country*, that address being the focus of one part of the New York Society the novel describes. But Wharton's attitudes to Europe and European culture are balanced with much more obvious irony, and indeed criticism, than James displays; her concerns are more social and moral than aesthetic. And the simple fact that her novels were serialized makes the readability factor much more pressing than in later James.

However, it is vital to trace in Wharton what her own characteristics are, over and above the clear references to the tradition she sees herself in. She anticipates Virginia Woolf in her concern for 'a room of one's own', the female writer's space in society. She was, of course, rich enough not to have to struggle with poverty, and she had an immense admiration for someone like George Eliot or George Sand who did manage to struggle from obscurity to the realization of her talent. Coincidentally, both of these great nineteenth-century women writers felt it necessary to take male names in order to achieve their goals in writing. Edith Wharton's talent lay dormant for many years, in the becalmed waters of her marriage to Teddy, which ended just at the time of *The Custom of the Country*. The struggle in her case was not against poverty, but against boredom, and the suffocation of a society with no interest in art or creativity.

What Edith worked on most assiduously in the early years of her creative career was the interior design of houses, and this is one of the most significant influences on all her writing. Her first published book was *The Decoration of Houses*, in 1897, a hugely influential volume which was still in print forty years later. As Shari Benstock puts it, 'the house as metaphor for woman became a dominant literary trope in her writing'. In one of her early stories, *The Fullness of Life*, we find this deservedly famous quotation:

I have sometimes thought that a woman's nature is like a great house full of rooms: there is the hall through which everyone passes going in and out; the drawing room, where one receives formal visits; the sitting-room where members of the family come and go as they list; but beyond that, far beyond, are other rooms, the handles of whose doors perhaps are never turned; no one knows the way to them, no one knows whither they lead; and in the innermost room, the holy of holies, the soul sits alone and waits for a footstep that never comes.

There are echoes of Bluebeard here, but the woman's territory is uncharted, unexplored. That is where Edith Wharton would find the material for her greatest novels. In her novels, Edith Wharton opens these doors, to areas of woman's experience which had not been written about before, and more specifically, had not been written about by women. If Undine Spragg is criticized as a schemer, unfeeling and utterly selfish, it has to be argued that such *male* characters had appeared in dozens of novels. Was woman to remain the eternal feminine, the 'angel in the house' as the Victorians might have wanted?

Wharton's female characters, especially in the New York novels, *The House of Mirth*, *The Custom of the Country* and *The Age of Innocence,* and in some her best shorter stories like *Madame de Treymes* (which is close in many of its themes to *The Custom of the Country*) are not necessarily *nice* women. George Eliot, at the very end of *Middlemarch,* famously gives society's judgement on the heroine, Dorothea, by those who did not know her: 'she could not have been a "nice" woman'. Of course the reader knows all her positive sides as well as the negatives that might have led to such a social judgement. But the ambivalence of society's ways of judging women is crucial. Thomas Hardy called Tess in *Tess of the d'Urbervilles* 'a pure woman' (it is the sub-title of the novel), in fact, deliberately provoking readers into having to judge the flawed and ambivalent character in a more rounded and considered way.

So Wharton places herself in a tradition of examining women's motivations and behaviour, *and the judgements on them.* It is clear that many of the judgements of Undine Spragg do demonstrate some kind of double standard: scheming ambivalent heroes have flourished in novels from Henry Fielding (*Jonathan Wild* comes to mind) to the present day (Tom Wolfe's 1987 masterpiece *The Bonfire of the Vanities* has many echoes of the upwardly mobile New York aspirations of Undine Spragg). But when a woman does similar things to these male fictional heroes, she is judged rather more harshly, as indeed Emma Bovary or Tess were. Undine Spragg is *not* a nice woman, nor is she meant to be.

Edith Wharton was not an experimentalist, but she does foreshadow many techniques which would appear in modernist fiction. Malcolm Bradbury refers to both Joseph Conrad in Britain and Stephen Crane in America in the late 1890s as the initiators of the movement which came to be defined as Modernism. He quotes Conrad's Preface to *The Nigger of the 'Narcissus'* (1898), which stated, 'My task which I am trying to achieve is, by the power of the written word to make you feel – it is, before all, to make you see.' Wharton believed in traditional literary values of 'order' and beauty, and can be seen as straddling two styles of novel-writing as well as two continents. For where America had become, as Hegel had put it, 'the land of the future', it was also a land without a past, so anyone who dared to write about it was caught between the past and the future, between the *mimesis* of direct realism and the fragmentation, the fracturing of cultural types and icons, genres and structures. As Bradbury says, 'it was a world beyond the tired historical dialectic of Europe', and although Wharton cannot be seen as fully associating with those Moderns who 'dissolved the forms and consciousness of the past', she is clearly probing the future, balancing tradition with the need in Ezra Pounds' famous words to Make It New.

Wharton gives great importance to dialogue, and frequently presents long stretches of dialogue without naming the characters, simply allowing them to speak for themselves. She affirmed in *The Writing of Fiction* (1925), 'Dialogue in fiction should be reserved for the culminating moments and regarded as the spray into which the great wave of narrative breaks in curving towards the watcher on the shore.'

Many of the climactic moments in *The Custom of the Country* confirm her success in this: the dialogues between Elmer and Undine in Chapter XLI, and between her and Raymond de Chelles in Chapter XLII, for example.

She is also very modern in her movement in and out of the characters' thoughts: her use of Free Direct and Free Indirect Speech/Thought are highly significant in allowing the reader to penetrate into character and motive: contrast how Raymond is presented with how the narrator flits in and out of Undine's mind, for example.

But in some other ways Wharton is a traditionalist. She never allows much sexuality to emerge explicitly, although suggestions peep through now and again: Ralph's possible creativity 'in his veins' might suggest the displacement of sexual feelings to the modern reader, but clearly sexuality is not part of Wharton's subject matter. Psychology is, however. And she wants to go deep into the psychology of her characters, especially of Undine, although the result is that we perceive how shallow Undine actually is. It is part of Wharton's achievement that she can keep such a lengthy and complex plot spinning around a character who is fundamentally one-dimensional, and is such not because of the author's lack of imagination, but because of her own limitations.

Wharton spoke and wrote the 'Queen's English' rather than 'American', using British spelling and punctuation. This caused some negative reactions in America, being considered affected by some; one or two early critics even tried to remind her of American usages. However, this is indicative of the traditions she places herself in, and is part of the ambivalence of the whole America/Europe nexus of the novel. She gained her wealth from America, but she found her true home in France. She criticized the manners and *mores* of both societies, and berated both societies for their hypocrisies. This very ambivalence gives critics and readers their greatest scope for commentary and discussion.

In *The Custom of the Country*, marriage is a means to an end, brutally and explicitly so. It may have been the same in the novels of Jane Austen, but here the ambition and single-mindedness of Undine is not mitigated by charm. She is American beauty, yes, but she is also American ruthlessness and ambition, totally uncultured and without taste. It is very significant indeed that Elmer Moffatt, as the novel progresses, demonstrates growing cultivated tastes and aesthetic appreciation, although these will always be associated with his power to buy the admired objects. Undine has almost no redeeming features, and this is a vital part of Wharton's achievement in the novel. Undine Spragg is a totally modern anti-heroine, using all the best of her femininity in the most unscrupulous ways possible. She takes to a highest point, a kind of *non plus ultra*, the scheming heroine, Becky Sharp, in William Makepeace Thackeray's *Vanity Fair*, or the character she is closest to, Rosamund Vincy in *Middlemarch*. Both these characters are in some way redeemed by the end of the novel. Wharton does not apologize for Undine, redeem her, or excuse or mitigate her behaviour in any way. She simply shows her as she is – that seems to be both her achievement and her critical problem.

Edith Wharton herself justified her approach to Undine and her society in her autobiography, *A Backward Glance* in 1934: 'A frivolous society can acquire dramatic significance *only through what its frivolity destroys*. Its tragic implication lies in its power of debasing people and ideals.' Undine thrives at the expense of what she destroys: her parents, Ralph Marvell, her son. The novel is their tragedy, just as much as it is Undine's success story.

Undine's character and behaviour are not explained by heredity, by psychology, or indeed by anything. Just as Elmer Moffatt appears from nowhere 'one day behind the counter' at the wonderfully named Luckaback's Dollar Shoe-store in Apex (p. 309), Undine's character leaves her parents, and indeed the narrator, puzzled as to how it happened, where it came from. This can be read as simply a splendid metaphor for the inexplicability of the new phenomenon of burgeoning American-ness.

Undine receives no punishment in the novel, apart from the ups and downs of her marital and social progress. It is perhaps this lack of explicit moral judgement or come-uppance that leaves many readers and critics perplexed. In other novels, Wharton would give the leading character a foil, someone to contrast her behaviour and represent an alternative moral stance. But the ironic, brittle tone of this novel makes it clear from the outset that we are dealing with a character who is outside the normal scope of traditional values. She might be judged by conventional terms, but is not going to be swayed by anything she does not see as being to her own advantage. Only male characters have been allowed to get away with this for centuries in novels – Undine Spragg is highly unusual in that she gets away with it all the way through this novel. And at the end she is going on with her inexorable progress. Elmer might be her next victim, although the reader will probably feel that in more ways than one Undine has met her match in him.

Critical Reactions

The ways in which Undine displays herself and her identity are the object of a lot of comment, contrasting her obscure origins and her highly visible social career. For Lorna Sage, Undine Spragg is simply 'the latest incarnation of the frontier spirit'. For others it is her manipulation of New York Society that matters. For Maureen E. Montgomery the character 'takes the management of visibility to new extremes' and foreshadows the publicity-led lifestyles that became more and more familiar throughout the twentieth century. She adduces this as one main reason for the lack of sympathy for Undine. In the scene at the opera for instance (Chapter V) she is 'careful not to make herself a pushover for Van Degen . . .' but is 'an active female spectator who resists being appropriated by an avaricious, opportunistic male gaze'. This is in some ways indicative of how it is the female character who directs the course of the novel rather than any of the male characters, although Montgomery also says that 'Wharton offers us a very pessimistic reading of women's agency, of the extent to which women are able to determine either their own fate or the manner in which they wish to be read in relation to the dominant discourse of femininity'. It is worth quoting Montgomery's observations on this aspect of Wharton's discourse strategies:

One further point can be made in order to underscore the significance of Edith Wharton's fictional construction of women and discourse of femininity and her representation of what might be referred to as the 'new staging' of female bodies. . . . On one level at least, Wharton's novels can be read as a 'counter-discourse,' particularly to the consumer-oriented capitalist discourse of mass-circulation daily newspapers and weekly magazines associated with the conspicuous display of leisure and consumption by the nouveaux riches. Her novels attempt to deglamorize this class and to reveal the increasing sexual objectification of women in the competitive display of male wealth. Wharton exposes the gap between how her female characters believe they are presenting themselves to a public audience and how men in that audience view them – something newspapers cannot do because it goes against their self-interest. In doing so, Wharton underlines the dominant scopic regime that privileges men and problematizes women's role; not only in a class that seeks to visually overwhelm spectators with signs of its wealth, but also more generally in a consumer capitalist culture that deploys women's bodies in the commodification of glamor, luxury and leisure.

This very neatly brings together influences from Thorstein Veblen's seminal work *The Theory of the Leisure Class* (1899) and recent feminist approaches to text. Veblen's work observes 'quasi-predatory business habits' of the kind exemplified in *The Custom of the Country*, and sees them as 'reflections of the barbarian temperament'. His conflict explores Wharton's two sides, the Aborigines and the Invaders – both Veblen in his hugely influential book and Wharton in her novels are exemplifying Darwinism in its American manifestations. Benstock holds Wharton up as a convinced and well-read follower of Charles Darwin's theories of evolution.

Wharton is the major novelist of this leisured class that Veblen describes. The criticisms he makes of American capitalism are precisely the deep waters into which Wharton takes her fiction. Andrew Hook says that 'Veblen is important not as a prophet of the future of American society, but as an analyst of its present . . . [he] is able to cut through one assumption after another about American social attitudes and behaviour'. He goes on to speak of the famous image of 'the figure of Henry Frick, an immensely rich steel magnate, seated within his splendid New York home on a superb Renaissance throne beneath a priceless Renaissance baldacchino, reading a copy of the *Saturday Evening Post*. Such a conjunction of financial power, leisure, conspicuous consumption and tastelessness' might be the very starting point for Edith Wharton's novel, begun only a decade after Veblen's theory was published.

If we take this issue together with the familiar question of 'whether women writers produce texts which are significantly different in terms of language from those of males,' as Sara Mills affirms, we can see that *The Custom of the Country* can offer opportunites for argument from several points of view. Sara Mills, in *Feminist Stylistics*, usefully cites Virginia Woolf, Hélène Cixous and Luce Irigaray in her attempts to evaluate whether there is such a thing as 'women's writing'. Interestingly, Sandra M. Gilbert and Susan Gubar in their classic discussion of monstrous women in fiction (*The Madwoman in the Attic*) do not mention Wharton at all, although she would undoubtedly fit in many ways into their category of the 'nineteenth century literary imagination'. Sara Mills reminds us that 'phallocentrism is the practice of placing the male at the centre of theoretical models, and assuming that "male" is in fact coterminous with "human". As Monique Wittig says: "there are not two genders. There is only one: the feminine; the masculine not being a gender. For the masculine is not the masculine but the general."'

Whether or not we wish to read *The Custom of the Country* as rebelling against phallocentric Victorian texts, and as creating a modern female monster, it is worth comparing how male and female critics have read the text. Maureen E. Montgomery, for instance, reaches the rather unremarkable conclusion that 'at least as far as gender relations are concerned, Wharton's novel delivers a powerful critique of modern society and its sham claim to progressiveness. Wharton's achievement was to show how little had actually changed for women. This was not a popular message at a time when women had high hopes that they would soon be able to participate fully in the public world.'

Wharton has been remarkably little analysed by feminist critics. Carol Wershoven picks up the Gilbert/Gubar idea of the 'monstrous' woman, quoting Undine as the 'monstrously perfect result of the system', as she is described in the novel (p. 120). Trading, dealing in husbands and trading off her son for her freedom, are seen as the female's revenge, in a society where 'all the romantic values are reversed'.

Elaine Showalter draws many parallels with the career of the late-twentieth-century American entrepreneur, Donald Trump, and illuminates the novel with her references to what he called in his book, with its remarkably post-Darwinian title *The Art of Survival*, 'the Lucky Sperm brigade', the people born to wealth and power, 'unattractive people who often have done nothing smarter than inherit somebody else's wealth'. Trump could have been describing the society of Wharton's New York novels.

For Elizabeth Ammons this is 'one of America's great business novels', which seems to be a rather limiting judgement. Cynthia Griffin Wolff argues that by being this kind of novel, it is about a world of male captains of industry and thus, 'a saga of active men and passive women'. This seems to deny the very power and energy that drives Undine – passive is not the first adjective that comes to mind to describe her. Wolff goes on, 'this is an epic for men only and Undine cannot live in it . . . [She] has been debarred from the victory by reasons of sex'. This begs the whole question of how much Undine is victorious or vanquished. Certainly she is in her element at the end of the book, making use of Elmer's money for her social aims, as she has done all the way through, using her father and all the other men she can, to provide her with the means to her own ends. To see her as *not* reaching her greatest potential is to assume that she has undiscovered depths and qualities which might help her to even greater heights, but Wharton gives us no clue to any such hidden depths and resources in Undine. What you see is what you get.

Blake Nevius holds an opposite view to Wolff's. Undine, he says, 'holds all the cards'. Carol Wershoven agrees, suggesting that 'because business is the only passionate experience left, Undine brings the excitement of the business deal into the drawing room. She makes herself into a valuable commodity to be traded in marriage.' Elizabeth Ammons concludes that she has 'her own stock exchange . . . in which she herself is the stock exchanged.' Wolff calls her 'the perfectly commercial item, able to simulate anything the purchaser desires'.

So, if business is at the heart of the novel, as most critics seem to suggest, what is the role of the four major male characters? For Wershoven they 'are the objects of Wharton's scorn'. For her, 'the irony and satire in this novel arise not from the contrast between Undine's shallow aims and the bolder ones of her husbands, but from the similarity of their ambitions. All the men in Undine's life – Ralph Marvell, Van Degen, de Chelles, Moffatt – want money, pleasure and status; all share Undine's values.' Wershoven finds 'considerable hypocrisy in this restrictive world . . . In transforming herself into the perfect commodity, Undine reveals the tawdriness of her men's desires and the essential cheapness of the world they inhabit. Rather than tempt her lovers away from their society, Undine invades it, triumphs in it, and this exposes it for what it is.' Critics find there is 'no moral center within the world of the novel', as Cynthia Griffin Wolff, among others, says. It is a story of how much is lost in gaining the world. It is not pointed out that this in itself could be taken as a highly moral centre, and as a highly significant point which the reader must take away from the novel.

R. W. B. Lewis, Wharton's best biographer before Shari Benstock, points out that 'each of Undine's marriages is no more than another mode of imprisonment; and Undine's creator allows more than a hint that the young woman is as much a victim as an aggressor amid the assorted snobberies, tedium, and fossilised rules of conduct of American and, even more, French high society'. It is rare for a critic to see Undine as a victim herself, for she never questions any of the values of the society she wants to join. It is simply there, and she must conquer it. Were she to have questioned these values, there might be more possibility of sympathizing with her. For one critic, Janet Malcolm, Edith Wharton was 'the woman who hated women', and her creation of Undine is a manifestation of that hatred. She finds in Wharton 'a deep pessimism and equally profound misogyny', and goes so far as to describe Undine as the character with which 'Wharton takes her cold dislike to a height of venomousness previously unknown in American letters'.

The lack of passion is worth bringing in here. As Lorna Sage says in her introduction to the Everyman edition of the novel, 'Undine is never awoken sensually, hence her indignant conviction of her own innocence.' For Cynthia Griffin Wolff, 'the women all seem more hideously disfigured than their male counterparts in the money game' – a judgement that merits consideration in terms of the double standards question. Is Undine 'disfigured' by her ambitions, or are they merely the parallel text to Elmer's ambitions, which are realized in the open cut and thrust of business?

The business side of things could be seen as the legitimization of ambition – in which case Undine is the illegitimate, unacceptable face of that; by that token she will be judged more negatively than any of the men. For Janet Malcolm, Undine is all negative: 'stripped of all charm, spirit and warmth, the adventuress pared down to her pathology, but a pathology that is invested with a kind of magical malignancy'.

It might be argued that this is an example of 'man-made language', in feminist terminology, being used against the female 'monster'. But there is no point in criticizing a monster for being what it is – Wharton was, however, criticized for this from day one in the American press: 'she has constructed an ideal monster', wrote the New York *Sun* in October 1913, and the *New York Times Review of Books* found Undine 'the most repellent heroine we have encounterd in many a long day – so "monstrous" that at times she seems scarcely human, yet so cleverly portrayed that she is always real'.

There has often been comment on this pull between 'realism' and the artifice that satire implies. Is the character-drawing caricature, or is it realistic? 'Human nature as reflected in the pages of this novel is (n)ever particularly attractive,' the *Sun* had said. F. M. Colby in the *North American Review*, the following spring wrote, 'Disagreeable persons are never condemned or brought obviously to ridicule.' This lack of Victorian moralizing is part of what the present-day reader may consider the novel's greatness. Edith Wharton avoids obvious outright condemnations. Perhaps her characters have become more familiar to us now than they were to the original readers. Perhaps these original readers did not want to admit how many such ‘monsters’ there actually were in their midst.

One English reviewer, on the other hand, when the book was first published, found the ‘heroine a natural and pathetic figure’ and did in fact feel sympathy for her. But this is an unusual response. Others preferred to read it as ‘a parable’ and a ‘warning’.

Henry James’s first reactions to the novel take us back to the masculine–feminine question. He found ‘the masculine conclusion tending . . . to crown the feminine observation’, whatever that might mean. He found the novel ‘almost scientifically satiric’ – again a judgement which leaves us wondering what he meant.

Q. D. Leavis brings references to George Eliot, as we saw earlier, and even to Jane Austen into her judgement of *The Custom of the Country*. She discusses Austen in the context of what she calls ‘the common code of her society’ and decides it is a society where ‘manners . . . are seen to be based on moral values’, whereas ‘Mrs Wharton’s people are all primitives or archaic survivals’. Again, this is not necessarily to say that Edith Wharton was unaware of the moral vacuum at the heart of the society she is describing. True, she knew the society well, and was born into it, but Leavis seems to imply that the book lacks a moral core because its characters lack that same moral code and core. Readers must beware of imposing a moral code from outside on a novel which deliberately does not prescribe one.

Looking forward to later writers in the twentieth century, we can see that the emptiness at the heart of society is to become a wholly familiar subject. Indeed it was anticipated by Joseph Conrad in *Heart of Darkness* as early as 1902. Critics have seen Wharton’s novel as paving the way for the likes of Sinclair Lewis’s 1922 novel *Babbitt*. Elaine Showalter also relates Undine to the heroine of Margaret Mitchell’s *Gone with the Wind*, Scarlett O’Hara. The wholly or partially unlikeable hero or heroine was a new departure in fiction, and the risk that Wharton took in creating Undine was the risk of losing sympathy both for the heroine and for the novel. Edmund Wilson usefully points this out when he says that Undine is ‘the prototype in fiction of the “gold-digger”, of the international cocktail bitch’. What was remarkable in 1913 had become a commonplace by the time *Dynasty* hit the world's television screens in the 1970s and 1980s.

Recent perceptions of wealth and power in the 1980s and 1990s perhaps give us the chance to re-evaluate Edith Wharton's achievement in creating such a very modern heroine. She was certainly ahead of her time in terms of how readers would react to Undine, but the type she draws is as actual now as Thorstein Veblen suggested it was more than a century ago. Wharton, the artist, was observing what Hamlet calls 'the form and pressure of the time', and in so doing she created a heroine who has become more and more recognizable in the eighty and more years since the novel was completed.

Cynthia Griffin Wolff describes *The Custom of the Country* as 'Wharton's most ambitious masterpiece', but then she immediately brings in the negative perspective, 'it is a difficult and disorienting novel'. She rightly points out that 'the final judgement of any individual must be ambiguous'. She notes positively the novel's preoccupation with 'energy' and forward movement, which are very much themes of the twentieth century. It is, as Wolff suggests, a novel about ending as well as beginning, the twilight of one kind of society and the dawning of the most materialistic society the world has known. The custom of the country is self-gratification, not just divorce. The country is not just America or France, but is the old country and the new country, a question of generations as well as of nationality, of *arrivistes* as well as dinosaurs, of materialism and lack of spirituality. The novel, Wolff concludes, is 'a money novel, a business novel, that is true. However, above all, it is a novel of energy, of initiative.'

For Elizabeth Ammons, Undine's 'behaviour and her assimilated values reflect Wharton's criticism less of the parvenu than of the established American upper class, which in her view, as in Veblen's, is looked at as the ideal by all of American culture and thus epitomizes pervasive American attitudes (if not practices) towards women. That is, Edith Wharton *uses* Undine to reveal her criticism of the attitudes implicit in leisure class marriage.' Ammons finds not one of the characters admirable, which seems to be a common view. Not even Undine's parents escape criticism: even Mrs Spragg is seen as selfish.

Candace Waid sees art as a theme, saying that the novel 'represents a powerful vision of the impossiblity of art in America', which may seem contradictory given the artistic achievement of Wharton herself in her chosen art form.

Taken together, the main concerns of the criticism of the novel seem to be a negative consideration of the heartlessness and selfishness of all the characters, and a dissatisfaction with the lack of sentimentality or of concessions to rational morality in the novel.

These could alternatively be seen as praiseworthy, as indeed considerable attributes in a novel that is consciously breaking new ground. Some critics try too hard to see close autobiographical connections between Edith Wharton's own divorce and Undine's use of divorce to further her ends. Such criticism only serves to underline Wharton's achievement in creating in this novel a series of characters who represent the twentieth century even more clearly in the twenty-first century than they were recognized as doing in the century in which they were created.

Discussion Topics

Thesis/Antithesis: Writing about and Discussing *The Custom of the Country*

When discussing any literary text it is vital to balance your arguments in a for/against, pro/con manner, and work towards your own evaluation, which responds to the question or discussion topic posed.

Any examination is likely to want to evaluate the candidate in terms of

what has been learned
how that learning is applied in relation to the questions asked
how that learning is expressed.

This involves the exercise of several critical, analytical and discursive skills:

the ability to balance arguments and work towards a conclusion
the ability to select topic areas, and to quote and summarize constructively
the ability to make connections and cross-references
the ability to organize and present the material clearly
the ability to express the arguments concisely and correctly
the ability to take subjective viewpoints and justify them with objective criteria
the ability to contextualize.

In the case of *The Custom of the Country* there are several topic areas which might emerge:

comparison and contrast between American and French high society and the 'customs' of the two countries

questions of money and values
the relationship between business and divorce
the modernity of the characters and themes
the lack of sympathy of the characters
the absence of a 'moral core' to the novel
the relationship of the story to the life of the author
the aesthetic context of the novel
whether or not the feminine/masculine poles are significant (i.e. would it have been written differently by a man? etc.).

In any assignment, essay or answer, it is important to remember *there is no single correct response*. The quality of the individual response depends on clear thinking, the selection of lines and arguments to pursue, the relevant and appropriate use of quotations from or references to the text, and a balanced argument which is stated at the outset, discussed, and brought to a clear conclusion.

It is important not to be prescriptive, that is, not to assert any single or personal interpretation too forcibly, but to use modality in the balanced presentation of possible ways of thinking: 'it might be. . .', 'it could be read as . . .', 'this seems to suggest . . .' are much more useful than the present simple tense 'it is'.

As is clear from the brief selection of critical viewpoints on the text, debate rather than definitive pronouncement must be the response to this novel. Naturally, each individual reader will like or dislike the novel, will react individually, will want to pursue different lines and approaches within the text and outside the text. Your own reading, responses, reflections and whatever further reading you can do will all enrich your ability to answer any question about the text. Your reading frame of reference should be as wide as possible – this is part of 'what has been learned' – and it will be important to apply that learning appropriately to the rubric of the question or theme assigned. There is no point in knowing a great deal about the text, its context and what critics have said about it, if you do not respond appropriately and relevantly to what is asked. Selectivity is vital, therefore. The best readers will have a range of thoughts, of approaches, of possible responses to the text, not just one single line of interpretation or reading.

For this reason, further reading is recommended, especially of the Benstock biography. It will furnish more background than this series of notes can give. Further critical reading will confirm that there is no single, clear, definitive approach to this text (as with most good texts) – there are many ways of approaching it, and any individual reader might reject the ways it has been read here, and prefer to adopt another approach. It is important, however, as has been stressed repeatedly, not to let any single philosophy or theory dominate a reading of any text such as this. A purely feminist approach would be as misguided as a purely structuralist approach. The judicious balancing of possible approaches will be a positive sign of 'what has been learned' and 'how that learning can be applied'.

Above all, enjoyment of the novel is the best basis for a good solid confidence in discussing and evaluating it.

Further Discussion Points and Themes

What is, for you, the most significant 'custom of the country'?

How much is the book a 'masculine' novel or a 'feminine' novel?

Do you think Wharton favours one society (American or French) over the other, or are they equally satirized?

Compare and contrast the stratification and stultification of American and French society, as they are described in the novel.

How important are culture and aesthetic appreciation in the novel?

How much do you find the novel realistic in its characterization and plot?

Discuss the role of newspapers and reportage in the novel.

Do the characters change and develop during the course of the novel?

One critic, Cynthia Griffin Wolff, finds 'perversity and constant change' the main quality of the novel. How much do you agree or disagree?

Elaine Showalter suggests that 'a male Undine Spragg would

not be a great tycoon'. Do you agree, or is this the wrong way to approach the character?

Lorna Sage says 'the apparently dominant position of the Undines of the American world is deceptive. The power stays with their spouses', and adduces Simone de Beauvoir's *The Prime of Life* to back her up, quoting her on the myth of 'castrating' American women: 'even if it is true that the spirit of revenge in her has been exasperated to the point of making her a "praying mantis," she still remains a dependent and relative being. America is a masculine world.' Is this confirmed by your reading of the novel?

Is the novel pessimistic and misogynistic, in your view? Or are these traits tempered by irony?

'Divorce is the (anti-)institution, the "custom", which enables private life to adjust to the pressures of the market, and divorce is the "fairy-tale" solution to the plot, in Wharton's comic world-turned-upside-down. Divorce symbolizes the new style of speculation in flesh.' (Lorna Sage) How much do you agree or disagree with this view?

How much is the novel about freedom and liberty, in your opinion?

Discuss the nature of 'frontiers' in the novel, both in the geographical and in the moral sense.

Write a review of the novel as you see it, in terms of literary achievement, social commentary and cultural perspectives.

Bibliography

References

Ammons, Elizabeth, *Edith Wharton's Argument with America*. Athens, University of Georgia Press, 1980.

Auchincloss, Louis (ed.), Introduction to *The Edith Wharton Reader*. New York, Scribner, 1965; New York, Collier Macmillan, 1989.

Benstock, Shari, *No Gifts from Chance: A Biography of Edith Wharton*. New York, Scribner, 1994; London, Penguin, 1995. (The best available biography: strongly recommended.)

Bradbury, Malcolm, *Dangerous Pilgrimages: Trans-Atlantic Mythologies and the Novel*. London, Martin Secker & Warburg, 1995; London, Penguin, 1996.

Gilbert, Sandra M. and Susan Gubar, *The Madwoman in the Attic: The Woman Writer and the Nineteenth-Century Literary Imagination*. New Haven, Yale University Press, 1979.

Griffin Wolff, Cynthia, *A Feast of Words: The Triumph of Edith Wharton*. New York, Oxford University Press, 1977.

Hook, Andrew, *American Literature in Context III: 1865–1900*. London, Methuen, 1983. (Chapter 13, pp. 178–90, is on Thorstein Veblen.)

Hutchinson, Stuart (ed.), *Edith Wharton: The House of Mirth*, *The Custom of the Country*, *The Age of Innocence*. Cambridge, Icon Critical Guides, 1998. (Chapter 3, pp. 76–102, contains a good range of contemporary reviews and critical response.)

Lewis, R. W. B., *Edith Wharton: A Biography*. New York, Harper & Row, 1975; London, Vintage, 1993.

Malcolm, Janet, 'The Woman Who Hated Women', in *New York Times Book Review*, 16 November, 1986.

Mills, Sara, *Feminist Stylistics.* London, Routledge, 1995. (Chapters 1–3, pp. 25–79 – 'Feminist Models of Text', 'The Gendered Sentence', and 'Gendered Reading' – are excellent on the subject of *écriture feminine.*)

Montgomery, Maureen E., *Displaying Women: Spectacles of Leisure in Edith Wharton's New York.* New York, Routledge, 1998. (Especially Chapters 5, 6, and Conclusion – pp. 134, 156, 161–2 and 163–9.)

Nevius, Blake, *Edith Wharton: A Study of Her Fiction.* Berkeley, University of California Press, 1953.

Roll, Millicent (ed.), *The Cambridge Companion to Edith Wharton.* Cambridge, Cambridge University Press, 1995. (Contains the article by Elaine Showalter, pp. 87–97.)

Sage, Lorna, Introduction to *Edith Wharton: The Custom of the Country*. London, Everyman's Library, 1994.

Showalter, Elaine, '*The Custom of the Country:* Spragg and the Art of the Deal', in Roll (ed.), *op.cit.* 1995, pp.87–97.

Spender, Dale, *Mothers of the Novel: 100 good women writers before Jane Austen.* London, Routledge & Kegan Paul, 1986.

Waid, Candace, *Edith Wharton's Letters from the Underworld: Fictions of Women and Writing*. Chapel Hill, University of North Carolina Press, 1991.

Wershoven, Carol, *The Female Intruder in the Novels of Edith Wharton.* London and Toronto, Associated University Presses, 1982.

Wilson, Edmund, *The Wound and the Bow.* London, W. H. Allen, 1941; London, Methuen, 1961. (Chapter 4, pp.174–190, is devoted to Edith Wharton.)

Other Editions

Edith Wharton's *The Custom of the Country* is also available in the following editions:

Berkley Books, New York, 1981, with an Introduction by Marilyn French.

Collier Macmillan, New York, 1987, with an Introduction by Cynthia Griffin Wolff.

Oxford University Press World's Classics, Oxford, 1995, with an Introduction by Stephen Orgel.

Everyman's Library, London, 1994, with an Introduction by Lorna Sage.

Virago, London, 1995, with an Introduction by Elaine Showalter.

Further Reading

Auchincloss, Louis (ed.), Introduction to *The Edith Wharton Reader*. New York, Scribner, 1965; New York, Collier Macmillan, 1989.

Baume, Dale M., *Edith Wharton's Brave New Politics*. Madison, University of Wisconsin Press, 1994.

Beer, Gillian, *Darwin's Plots: Evolutionary Narrative in Darwin, George Eliot and Nineteenth-Century Fiction*. London, Routledge & Kegan Paul, 1983.

Bloom, Harold (ed.), *Edith Wharton: Modern Critical Views*. New York, Chelsea House, 1986.

—, *The Western Canon*. New York, Harcourt Brace, 1994; London, Macmillan, 1995.

Carter, Ronald and John McRae (eds.), *Language, Literature and the Learner: Creative Classroom Practice*. London, Longman, 1996.

Costanzo Cahir, Linda, *Solitude and Society in the Works of Herman Melville and Edith Wharton*. Westport, Greenwood, 1999.

Elrich, Gloria C., *The Sexual Education of Edith Wharton*. Berkeley, University of California Press, 1992.

Fedorko, Kathy A., *Gender and Gothic in the Fiction of Edith Wharton*. Birmingham, University of Alabama Press, 1995.

Goodman, Susan, *Edith Wharton's Women: Friends and Rivals*. Cambridge, Massachusetts, Press of New England, 1990.

—, *Edith Wharton's Inner Circle (Literary Modernism)*. Austin, University of Texas Press, 1994.

Killoran, Helen, *Edith Wharton: Art and Allusion*. Birmingham, University of Alabama Press, 1995.

Massa, Ann, *American Literature in Context IV: 1900–1930*. London, Methuen, 1983.

McDowell, Margaret, *Edith Wharton*. New York, Twayne, 1990.

McRae, John, *Literature with a Small 'l'*. London, Macmillan/ Prentice-Hall, 1991/1997.

Preston, Claire, *Edith Wharton's Social Register*. New York, St Martin's Press, 2000.

Tintner, A. R. and A. Tintner (eds.), *Edith Wharton in Context: Essays on Intertextuality*. Birmingham, University of Alabama Press, 1999.

Vita-Finzi, Penelope, *The Female Intruder in the Novels of Edith Wharton*. London, Pinter, 1993.